Making
it as
a
Couple

Prescription for a Quality Relationship

Making
it as
a
Couple

Prescription for a Quality Relationship

Allen Fay, M.D.

FMC BOOKS • Essex, CT

PUBLISHER'S NOTE

This publication is designed to provide accurate and authoritative information in regard to the subject matter covered. It is sold with the understanding that the publisher is not engaged in rendering psychological, medical, or other professional services. If expert assistance or counseling is needed, the services of a competent professional should be sought.

Library of Congress Cataloging-in-Publication Data

Fay, Allen.
Making it as a Couple:
prescription for a quality relationship / Allen Fay.
226 p.   cm.
Originally published: New York : Multimodal Press, c1988.
Includes bibliographical references.
ISBN 0-9659818-0-0
1. Marriage. 2. Interpersonal relations.   1. Title
HQ734.F33   1994   97-61526
646.7'8--dc20

This book was originally published under the title *PQR: Prescription for a Quality Relationship*. Minor editing changes have been made by the author, but the information in this edition is the same.

Printed in the USA
Book design by Richard Feinman
Cover design by Margaret Morgan

Copyright © 1988, 1994, 1998
by Allen Fay, M.D.

Published by
FMC BOOKS
P.O. Box 275
Essex, Connecticut 06426

Contents

FOREWORD

Why read this book? How does it differ from the plethora of self-help books, communication manuals, and other accounts that promise relationship enhancement and marital bliss? Besides, can a book really show you how to develop quality relationships in general, and how to transform a dull or conflict-ridden one in particular? In this instance, the answer on both counts is *yes*.

Making it as a Couple differs from all other works of its kind by providing specific recipes, easy to follow prescriptions, and precise methods that have an immediate impact. You won't have to wade through boring theories or work hard to find effective tactics and strategies. Virtually every page has creative solutions that give constructive power to your interpersonal dealings.

As a professor and as a therapist, I have used previous drafts of the book in my classes and with my clients. Even the very first rough draft led me to exclaim "This stuff is fantastic!" Each revision made it better and better. My feelings of excitement and enthusiasm about *Making it as a Couple* are shared by colleagues, students and numerous clients who have applied Dr. Fay's recommendations.

A quality relationship is one that avoids the pitfalls of conflict, coercion and control. It embodies the best features of respect, dignity, and consideration. A skillful communicator acquires a secure sense of strength and confidence that promotes trust and goodwill. *Making it as a Couple* shows exactly how to avoid inflammatory reactions, how to circumvent power struggles, and how to phrase requests, suggestions, observations, and objections so that they are understood and respected. The book provides tools for action, marshals skillful responses, and furnishes intelligent solutions. Typists, editors, and others who have been exposed to *Making it as a Couple* spontaneously volunteered that they had derived enormous benefit.

In the field of human relationships, the all too common "do-as-I-say-not-as-I-do" philosophy is unacceptable. Allen Fay is an exemplar of the methods he advocates. He does exactly what he advises us to do. This book comes from the pen (word processor) of a gifted psychiatrist who is first and foremost a compassionate human being, and whose special talent for successful relationships can now be acquired by anyone who reads *Making it as a Couple* and puts its principles into practice.

Arnold A. Lazarus, Ph.D.
Distinguished Professor Emeritus
Graduate School of Applied
  and Professional Psychology
Rutgers University

PREFACE

Making it as a Couple is based on my professional experiences as a psychiatrist working with individuals, couples and families for more than 30 years, and it comes also from the many things I have learned in my personal relationships. Although it is written for couples, it is also for singles who would like to be coupled and, in fact, it can benefit anyone who is having difficulty creating or maintaining any kind of relationship. The same basic principles and exercises have been used successfully with friends, relatives, neighbors, business associates, and even in larger social and political arenas (labor-management interactions, international diplomacy).

This book is written about real people and real problems, and as a result many of the examples reflect the sexist biases of our culture. Our model is the adult heterosexual couple, but, because the message of the book is for all relationships, the word "partner" is used frequently.

I am extremely fortunate in having learned as much as I did from my friends, family, colleagues and partners. Some of the lessons were quite painful, others less so. A debt of gratitude is due particularly to the following people, who contributed in some way to my understanding of the subject, provided me with partnership experience, offered encouragement and support, made invaluable editorial suggestions or brought great energy and skill to the typing of seemingly infinite versions and revisions of the manuscript:

Connie Bassett; Aaron Beck; Robin Distance; Celeste Edell; Albert Ellis; Harold Fay; Helen Fay; Julie Fay; Jeffrey Feinman; Richard Feinman; Jay Haley; Laura Haney; Kathryn Lance; Arnold Lazarus; Patricia MacMenamie; Gerald Patterson; Ann Marie Plaia; Susana Posadas; Jacqueline Ryzman; Sandra Simms; Richard Stuart; and Carl Whitaker.

Finally, I want to express my gratitude to the many patients who shared their problems with me and taught me so much about relationships.

Part One
Introduction

Is your relationship on the rocks? Or is it just stale? Perhaps it's even pretty good, but you feel it could be better. The fact is that most relationships don't work. Either they don't work at all, they don't work for long or they don't work very well. They certainly don't work as well as they might. Why not? The simplest answer is that most couples don't know how to make them work. The majority of us go through life without the necessary skills for creating and maintaining quality relationships.

Making it as a Couple will help you develop these skills and make your relationship as good as it can possibly be by using the same techniques that have helped so many couples in my office. By applying these ideas, which are based on modern communication psychology, you will see how an unsuccessful relationship can be improved in a short time, even after years of unhappiness.

Successful relationships occur for two basic reasons: Good Matching, where you and your partner start out with compatible dispositions, habits and interests; and Good Managing, that is, what you do with the raw materials. If you have a partner, you have already done the matching part—for better or worse. *Making it as a Couple*, therefore, is mainly about good managing. If you don't have a partner, the book can help you with any future relationship.

Managing your relationship better requires some effort and planning, but the rewards are well worth it. To succeed, all you need are three ingredients: MOTIVATION, AWARENESS, and TOOLS. Since you are already reading the book, you are off to a good start with MOTIVATION. Part Two focuses on developing an AWARENESS of the things you do (we'll call them TRAPS) that may be interfering with your own happiness. And Part Three offers an arsenal of TOOLS to reverse the deterioration or stagnation that is making your relationship less than it can be.

Before getting to the heart of the book, the TRAPS and the TOOLS, let's consider your options. If you are in a distressed relationship, you have four alternatives:

1) Accept it for what it is;
2) Suffer and resent it;
3) End the relationship;
4) Work at making it better.

This book is about option four. It pinpoints habit patterns that interfere with happiness and also provides the tools to improve almost any relationship. Ending the relationship is also reasonable in cases where there is a gross mismatch, where the relationship was never satisfactory, or where there are irreconcilable positions about major issues (e.g., one partner must have a child to be fulfilled, the other will not have a child under any circumstances). There is no shame in recognizing and accepting the fact that you made a mistake and are simply not suited to each other. What I find most distressing about couples breaking up is that many people genuinely want to get along better but just don't how.

It Will Never Work, So What's the Point of Trying

People who are unhappy in their relationships often express this feeling. If you are not sure that you want to continue the relationship but you choose to live with your partner for another month or even another day, why not make it as tolerable as possible? If you decide to end it, you are free to do so. But for the time that remains until you can muster the strength or make the necessary arrangements, why continue to be miserable? Why not use the next day or week or month to practice skills that will help you become a more effective communicator and partner, for future relationships if not this one. Even if you start getting along better, you are not obligated to stay together. On the other hand, you might realize that you can *make it as a couple* after all.

There is great power in relationships when the intellect, talent and energy of two people can be brought to bear on the problems that life deals us. **If we devoted a fraction of the time, effort and thought to improving our relationships that we do to our work or to our leisure time interests, the results would be electrifying.** Isn't it odd that we don't apply more thought to our major relationship, which has the potential for providing enormous pleasure, satisfaction and contentment, or reducing us to pain, despair and futility? Operating as a team rather than as parallel partners or adversaries is the best way to improve the quality of relationships. However, you will see shortly that, if necessary, *you can bring about changes in your relationship entirely on your own—without any help from your partner.*

Why YOU *Should Make The Effort*

If you are unhappy with your relationship, you probably feel that you're not getting as much as you're giving. It rarely happens that someone in my office says, "I really have a good deal. I get a lot more than I give." We are more likely to recite our own contributions and devalue those of our partner or think about what we are missing. A patient once said to me, "Marriage is a 50/50 proposition, isn't it?" I replied, "No, marriage is a 60/60 proposition. Each person has to do a little more than what he thinks his share is." I often hear partners say, "Why should *I* be the one to change? Why should *I* do all the work?" The answer is that the work you put into your relationship is not done for your partner's benefit. It is not even done for this relationship. It is done for

4

yourself! Practicing these exercises will help make you a more effective person in *any* relationship; it will help you be more confident, more tolerant, more assertive, more giving, more affectionate, more considerate. We expect that your present relationship will improve, but in any event, you will have practiced skills and learned something valuable that you can bring to other relationships. A relationship is, among other things, a vehicle for personal growth. Therefore, any effort that you put into it should not be resented, but rather viewed as an investment in yourself.

Relationships Involve Two People

This might seem obvious; yet many think that their unhappiness is caused solely by their partner. They act as if the relationship would be better if their partner alone changed. Relationship problems are always two-person problems that usually require two-person solutions. If you say to your partner, "I'm fine, the problem is with you" or, "When you get your act together, maybe then we can work things out," you are on a road that will probably lead nowhere. *We*, the couple, need to look at and change what *we* are thinking, saying and doing. Instead of observing and reacting to your partner as an individual, you will see how important it is to look at the couple, the two-person unit, what communications specialists call the *system*.

You Are A Chooser, Not A Victim

You are in this relationship by choice. It is important to recognize that you are a decision maker. You have options and alternatives. There are always other partners, other lifestyles, other standards of living. Clearly some choices are hard to make, especially the decision to end a long standing relationship. There are many who choose to stay in relationships they loathe; others end relationships even though they have several children to support and no job, because they feel that they have a better chance of being happy. There are always options. Hardly anybody is really trapped and locked in without choices. This psychological concept is critically important. People who believe that they have little control over their own destinies are likely to have poorer physical and emotional health than those who realize that they have a choice. This statement is true even if they never actually change their situation.

'Til Death Do Us Part — But Was It Good?

Have you ever seen a television talk show or game show host ask an elderly couple how long they have been married, and, when the answer is "50 years," the host says, "Isn't that wonderful?" At this point the audience applauds. In truth, it might be wonderful and it might not. The fact that a relationship lasts doesn't mean that it is good. Many couples live together for 50 years in constant torment. Others have a wonderful life together for two, five or ten years, and then separate. If the relationship is good, it will probably last; but if it lasts, it isn't necessarily good. Durability and quality are very different.

Getting What You Want

From the day we are born, we try to satisfy our needs and desires, and we do this largely through relationships—and mainly by *communicating*. The basic purpose of communicating is to get something we want from others: companionship; affection; food; sex; money; agreement; approval; a sympathetic ear; sharing a beautiful experience or even a chance to give to someone.

Whether you get what you want depends on:

1) What you want (your needs, desires and expectations). The simpler your needs and the more modest your expectations, the easier it will be to find satisfaction in your relationship.

2) Your partner's capacity to give it to you. Some partners do not have the personality, the intellect, the financial resources or the sex drive to satisfy their mate's needs.

3) How you ask for it (directly, clearly, assertively or indirectly and unpleasantly).

4) What you provide for your partner that makes him or her receptive to your requests. Most relationships work best when there is reciprocity.

Although there are many reasons for relationship unhappiness and for the failure to get what you want, most problems in relationships are related in some way to inadequate or faulty communication. Some of the things you want may not be available because of a mismatch between your expectations and your partner's ability to provide what you want. However, the key to satisfying your wants is to be found in developing more skillful ways of communicating.

For our purposes, the communication process involves two people, a *sender* and a *receiver,* and it consists of two parts, the *expressive* component and the *interpretive* component. The expressive component is the statement that conveys your desires and feelings to your partner (e.g., "I love you," "Let's go to the movies," "You're a jerk."). It includes not only the words you speak but also your tone of voice, facial expression, posture and gestures. The *interpretive* component is the meaning you give to what your partner says and does (e.g., "He thinks I'm stupid," "She cares more about her sister than about me.").

These two parts of the communication process, the expressive and the interpretive—what is public and what is private, what goes on in the world and what goes on in your head, what you and your partner say and do, and how you interpret each other's words and actions, are the keys to a better relationship.

As you begin to work on your communication patterns, it is important to realize the big difference between *content* (*what* you say) and *style* (the *way* you say it). Sometimes a change in style alone will turn a relationship around. Often, however, specific content issues have to be discussed, negotiated and resolved. But, if your style is negative, it is hard to discuss, negotiate or resolve anything. If you don't know how to express your requests and feelings (style), the content will be lost. That is why one of the critical principles of communication is: **Style Precedes Content**.

Although sometimes there are issues that are non-negotiable, compromise is possible most of the time. Even if it isn't, a pleasant style makes living with your differences much more tolerable. It is especially sad to see how many couples agree on basic issues but are miserable because they don't know how to relate to each other. They are fine with content but terrible when it comes to style.

If you look at the results of the interactions you have with your partner, you will see that there are basically three types of communications: those that promote closeness; those that create distance; and those that do neither. It is important to send messages that make your partner feel closer to you and want to respond positively, and to avoid styles that drive him/her away and make it difficult to respond favorably. For example, if you want your partner to do the dishes, you have a better chance if you say, "Honey, would you do dishes tonight?" rather than, "Don't you think it's about time you did something around here besides watch television?" You might think that the friendlier way is obvious and should come naturally. Or, you might think, "It's not that important if you love each other." The better way of communicating may seem obvious when you are reading about it, but it doesn't come naturally and it is not obvious in millions of relationships that have soured. As for loving each other, all too often love and pain are closely related.

Consider another example. Betty has been feeling unloved for many months and would like Paul to say that he loves her. See if you think it matters which of the following statements she makes to him:

1) "You don't care about me."
2) "You never say you love me."
3) "Why don't you tell me you love me?"
4) "It means a lot to me when you tell me you love me."

Now see if you think it makes any difference which of the following statements she makes to *herself*:

1) "He doesn't love me."
2) "He knows how much it means to me.
   He would say it if he cared about me."
3) "He is a cold and mean person."
4) "I know he loves me. He shows it in other ways."

How would you react in this situation? In relationships that work best, partners are most apt to use response #4.

Introduction

How can a relationship improve in a short time when it has been a disaster for so many years? Psychologists know that frequently the simplest changes in your actions toward your mate can have an enormous and even lasting impact. To give an example of a simple remedy, suppose you and your partner have a miserable relationship that is filled with daily hostility and abuse. Let us say that you now agree to a one week truce. No matter what happens, whatever disappointments and irritations there are, you will not say a single hostile thing to each other for that one week period. Do you think that in any way at all your *relationship* will be better? Or, more simply, do you think that you will get along any better during *that week?* If in addition you agree to pay each other one compliment per day, would that help? "Maybe," you say, "But the basic feelings are still rotten." Now, if both of you avoid uttering a single hostile word to each other for a period of one month, and in addition you exchange one compliment per day, and what's more, you hug each other for one minute twice a day, is it possible that you will *feel* less angry, resentful and bitter toward each other? In other words, do you think it ever happens that *behavior change precedes feeling change?* I hope you do, because this principle is one of the cornerstones of modern psychological thinking and one of the secrets to *making it as a couple.* Of course, these exercises alone will not solve all of your problems, Usually there are specific *content* issues to be addressed, but there are some couples who need no more than a few style changes to bring about marked and lasting improvement in their relationship. And, with some practice, the combination of content and style approaches in Parts Two and Three is likely to make a significant difference in your relationship.

Now we are ready to answer the two practical questions about your relationship: what's wrong with it and how to make it better.

Part Two
Relationship Traps

INTRODUCTION

This section contains 54 common Relationship Traps. These are the damaging things you say or do or think that create bad feelings and make it difficult or impossible to *make it as a couple*. Although there is no limit to the ways that you can be destructive, these basic traps are situations I have encountered again and again in my practice and in my personal life.

Errors of *commission* are worse than errors of *omission*. That is, saying and doing harmful things is worse than failing to do positive things. The problem in all troubled relationships is too much punishment and/or not enough satisfaction, but much more damage is caused by negative actions and beliefs than by too little pleasure. That is why so much space is given to the traps, and why the first step is to get you

13

to stop acting destructively toward your partner — *regardless of what your partner is doing.*

In reading about these traps, you will see that some of them are similar, but each one is important. At the end of each description, you are asked if you are *aware* of committing the particular error. You are not asked *whether* you commit the error, but only whether you are *aware* of committing it. In all relationships, at least some of these traps exist some of the time. You are specifically *not* asked if your *partner* does these things. While reading this section, you may have a strong urge to say to your partner, "Listen to this. It describes you perfectly." Don't do it! The whole point is to become more aware of what *you* are doing as a first step toward making the relationship better. You will find that you do many of these negative things without realizing it and, as a result, you may not even know what is wrong, let alone what to do about it.

Curious people, particularly scientists, try to find out why we do the things we do — the causes of our actions. Where do these damaging habits come from? Why do we do things that cause us so much pain? Such "why" questions are interesting and important, but in the field of psychology, causes are often complex. There are so many influences and experiences that make us what we are, that these questions are frequently unanswerable. Despite this limitation, it is usually possible to *do* something about problems, even without knowing exactly when, why or how they came about. This practical approach takes a lot less time and is more fruitful than years of looking for ultimate causes.

In a more general way, we can say that most destructive habits of thought and action stem from four basic sources:

1) *Destructiveness due to ignorance.* We might say that these are the people who don't know any better. Many simply do not know how to communicate effectively, and it may be enough to show them what they are doing and how it can be done better. For example, some people who really do appreciate their partners never utter a word of praise, because they don't realize how important it is to show support. Destructiveness due to ignorance is remedied by information, and it is in this group that we find the bulk of therapists' "one-session cures," as well as the largest group of people who benefit from self-help books.

2) *Destructiveness as a learned habit.* This refers to habits that have developed through imitation and psychological conditioning. Often we know better but have trouble stopping. Sometimes we are unaware of psychological reasons for our actions. What is required here, in addition to factual information, is practicing new and more effective styles and the unlearning of negative habits. Many of the exercises in the book are addressed to this type of destructiveness.

3) *Destructiveness that is willful.* Although in my opinion this type is uncommon, there are some who consciously attempt to inflict harm and create distance. Sometimes they are uncomfortable about intimacy and want distance, or they may be retaliating for some real or perceived harm done by their partner, or they may actually derive pleasure from being destructive.

4) *Destructiveness related to biological factors.* Many destructive emotions and actions can be explained to a large extent by medical or psychiatric illness. For example, withdrawal from a partner may sometimes be associated with schizophrenia, depression, anemia, an underactive thyroid gland or chronic pain. Outbursts of anger and physical violence may at times be connected with the premenstrual syndrome, with a particular type of epilepsy or with an abnormal sensitivity to alcohol. These are just a few examples. Without appropriate medication or other biological treatment, some couples' problems cannot be solved no matter how many books they study or how many therapists they consult.

Before we get to the list of traps, remember that you and your partner are a *two-person unit.* You are always dealing with one party's *action* and the other party's *reaction,* a behavior *and* a perception, one's error in sending messages and the other's error in receiving them. Sid frequently stares at other women when he is with Hannah, and she gets upset. Their relationship will work better if he doesn't look so much *and* if she doesn't take it so personally. Again, there will be no benefit if you focus on what your partner is doing rather than on what you are doing. The purpose of this section is to make you more aware of what *you* are doing.

1. RECITING PAST GRIEVANCES

Don't bring up negative experiences from the past, especially unpleasant things your partner did to you:

- "You got drunk on our wedding night and I'll never forgive you."
- "I remember how you insulted my sister."
- "You wouldn't have a child and now I'm too old."

While some incidents seem trivial and others are much more important, the essential thing to remember is that **The Past Is Dead.** It has value in only two ways:

1) Recalling *pleasant* experiences;
2) Learning from mistakes.

Rehashing old unpleasantness creates distance and causes resentment. If a deed was bad enough for you to end the relationship, by all means do so. But if you choose to stay with your partner, tell yourself to forget it, and don't hassle your mate. I say *forget* rather than forgive. Forgetting is much better than forgiving. Forgiving means that your partner was wrong and you are right. This maneuver puts you in a morally superior position, and that in itself causes trouble.

If your partner has done you some injustice in the past, either forget it or see if you can get some benefit in the present. If you want your partner to make up to you in some way for the hurt, ask pleasantly for what you want. There are two parts to the problem:

1) *Expressing* your resentment;
2) *Feeling* resentful.

And there are 2 parts to the solution:

1) Stop talking about it;
2) Neutralize your bad feelings.

If you successfully control the urge to recite past grievances, there are six steps for dealing with the negative *feelings*:

1) Downgrade the significance of the event, especially if it was a single isolated occurrence.
2) Think of the positive things in your relationship.
3) Think of any role *you* may have played in the incident, possibly some provocation or failure to assert yourself.
4) Assume that your partner was not acting maliciously.
5) In a pleasantly assertive way, request some compensation from your partner for what was done to you, if this is possible.
6) Ask yourself what is accomplished by harboring resentment.

Liz's mother lived alone and had to have a serious operation. The doctors said she needed a couple weeks of recuperation before she could go back to her home and they recommended that she stay with Liz and Charlie. Even though Charlie had nothing against Liz's mother, he refused to let her stay with them. Liz's mother felt very hurt and Liz never stopped resenting Charlie for his insensitivity.

Using the six steps listed above, how could Liz have dealt with this situation more effectively ? Now think of any incidents about which you harbor resentment. List them.

_____

_____

_____

The approach spelled out here does not preclude discussing ongoing issues that have never been settled or taking steps to see that past hurts are not repeated; nor does it prohibit bringing up the past in a way that neutralizes your own bad feelings. If done without bitterness, it may be all right to say, "Sometimes I really feel bad about the affair you had five years ago and I'm trying hard to forget it."

People who harbor or express resentment from the past destroy what they could have in the present and future.

RECITING PAST GRIEVANCES

Are you aware of doing this ?

PARTNER A		PARTNER B	
YES	NO	YES	NO
☐	☐	☐	☐

2. DISAPPROVING

You cannot appreciate everything your partner does, no matter how hard you try. Total approval or acceptance is simply unrealistic. On the other hand, chronic disapproval is common in relationships that have soured. "I don't like your clothes, your table manners, your extravagance, your stinginess, your leaving the closet doors open, the way you talk to the children." The list goes on and on. Sometimes the disapproval is non-verbal, perhaps a frown or a sneer. If there are specific changes you would like your partner to make, that's fine, and there are constructive ways of asking for them. But verbal or non-verbal disapproval causes tension and resentment. **Request a change of habit in the future instead of expressing disapproval in the present.**

Pete and Amy are financially strapped because Pete buys almost anything he wants. Amy tells him frequently that she disapproves of his spending habits. She also criticizes and blames him and compares him unfavorably to more frugal acquaintances. The destructive impact of his fiscal management style and her blatant disapproval was reversed when she asked in a pleasant way if major purchases could be discussed before they occurred. The couple decided to have weekly meetings to review finances. At the first meeting Pete agreed to discuss all purchases over fifty dollars and Amy agreed to avoid expressing disapproval. In addition, she downplayed his "relapses" and encouraged an ongoing constructive dialogue.

Just as important as eliminating disapproving statements is overlooking your partner's minor foibles and
learning how to tolerate habits that differ from your own.
Don't evaluate your partner's every action so that he/she
lives in constant fear of your disapproval.

DISAPPROVING
Are you aware of doing this ?

PARTNER A		PARTNER B	
YES	NO	YES	NO
☐	☐	☐	☐

3. CRITICIZING

Criticism is the basis for much learning and growing. We learn a great deal through comments we get from our partner, friends, family, teachers, children, neighbors, therapists and even strangers. But it is easy to fall into a routine of criticizing our partner's habits, beliefs, interests and handling of situations.

Because you may not be aware of falling into this trap, listen carefully for disparaging things you say to your partner, particularly negative "you" statements.

- "You are mean, stupid, hostile, incompetent..."

- "You aren't nice, bright, a good lover..."

- "You can't do anything right..."

Most of us don't want to be told what's wrong with us. However, criticism that is gentle, well intentioned and constructive, especially if it suggests changes for improving the relationship, can be invaluable. It is all right and even necessary to express negative feelings, but *requesting a change* is much better than criticizing. "Honey, I'd really appreciate your cleaning up" is better than "You're not very neat," or "You should clean up" (implied criticism). The latter statements don't lead to anything positive and are bound to cause problems.

CRITICIZING

Are you aware of doing this ?

PARTNER A		PARTNER B	
YES	NO	YES	NO
☐	☐	☐	☐

4. BLAMING AND SELF-JUSTIFYING

- "We got lost because you didn't get the directions straight."

- "Johnny got sick because you let him run out in the cold without a sweater."

- "We're overdrawn at the bank because you messed up the checkbook."

Many things go wrong in life and in relationships, and often it's difficult to accept or deal with these challenges. Straightening them out may require working together, but *blaming* makes this impossible. Laying the blame at your partner's feet rather than your own (or nobody's) may give your ego a temporary lift, but it is guaranteed to destroy your happiness.

"We lost the tennis match on account of your lousy playing." Even if it's true that you lost because your partner played badly, you will lose a lot more than a game if you blame her/him. Why is winning so important? And, what difference does it make whose fault it is? If your partner goofs, either say nothing, or, if you have a helpful suggestion for the future and can make your point in a benevolent, constructive way, ask for your partner's permission: "Honey, may I make a suggestion?" If the answer is negative, drop the subject. The answer to the tennis problem is:

don't play tennis with your mate or learn to downplay the importance of his/her performance on the court.

There are times when it is important to explain why things happened in order to avoid the same difficulty in the future, but remember that your goal is to create a no-fault relationship. **If something goes wrong, learn from it or forget it. It happened — Period.** Get on with your life.

Blaming is always bad, but it is particularly destructive to blame your partner for something he/she didn't do, or blame your partner for something that is your responsibility: "It's your fault that I'm fat because you bring food into the house." It is much better to accept responsibility for your own actions, e.g., "It's my responsibility that I overeat" or "I could have reminded you not to buy so much when you went shopping."

Make a particular effort to avoid partner-blaming that masquerades as self-blaming. It goes something like this: "I take full responsibility for what happened. It's entirely my fault, because I was too nice to you. I shouldn't have let you go back to school; now you think you're too smart for me."

Blaming goes hand in hand with another trap: self-justifying. "It was your fault we got lost; *I* wanted to bring a map." Or, "*You* misunderstood; *I* was perfectly clear." The maneuver of blaming your partner and justifying your own position is related to Traps #9 (Being Right) and #19

(Negative Comparisons) and strikes at the heart of a team approach to family life. The adversarial "Me vs. You" is incompatible with the collaborative "We" (we goofed), and it destroys your chance for closeness and happiness.

Working together to prevent what went wrong from happening in the future is much better than blaming and self-justifying. In cases where your partner *is* at fault, he probably feels bad enough already. Give him a little support, even if you were hurt by his actions.

Jane accidentally locks Bill out of the house. She is clearly in the wrong. If he blames her, he loses, she loses, they lose as a couple, and their kids lose because of the tension in the house. If, on the other hand, he says, "I know it was an accident, it's OK, no harm was done," the relationship will be a lot better. If Jane does this frequently, then Bill might say, "It's not serious and I know you feel bad about it. Let's see if we can work something out so it doesn't happen again."

BLAMING AND SELF-JUSTIFYING

Are you aware of doing this ?

PARTNER A		PARTNER B	
YES	NO	YES	NO
☐	☐	☐	☐

---

5. MAKING ACCUSATIONS

Whereas blaming lays the fault at your partner's feet when something has gotten fouled up, an accusation attacks your partner for something you don't like or feel is morally wrong. With both accusing and blaming, the statement may be factually correct but bringing it up, or the *way* it is brought up, is the problem. "You took my car without asking," and "You're having an affair with Sam," would be examples of accusations.

John went into the kitchen at 10 PM in search of a donut and found that there were none left. He didn't know what happened to them, but proceeded to bellow at Linda, "You ate all the donuts!!" Scientists know that shouting does not produce donuts. John's life is not improved in any way by accusing Linda. There are no donuts, whether he shouts or is pleasant. He can only upset, intimidate and alienate Linda by his angry assaults. It is better to solve the immediate problem (go out and buy more donuts or settle for something else). If this kind of thing happens often, propose a solution to the ongoing problem: "How about setting up a system so that the person who finishes the last can of soda or the ice cream or the donuts puts the item on a shopping list in the kitchen?"

MAKING ACCUSATIONS

Are you aware of doing this ?

PARTNER A		PARTNER B	
YES	NO	YES	NO
☐	☐	☐	☐

6. INTERROGATING YOUR PARTNER

"Where were you? Whom were you with? Why were you late? Who was that on the phone?" Don't grill your partner about her/his whereabouts, actions or motives, and particularly, don't interrogate your partner's family, friends or co-workers. Suspiciously asking children about what the other parent is doing is also very damaging, not only to your relationship but to your children. If you answer the phone and it's for your mate, excessive questioning of the caller is destructive, unless you've been asked to screen the calls.

Interrogating means mistrust, intrusiveness or an excessive degree of control over your partner. No one needs a district attorney on the home front. Instead of interrogating, show respect for your partner's privacy. Instead of "Where were you? Whom were you with?" you might try "Are you all right? Did you have a good time? I missed you. I'm happy to see you." It may be difficult at first but a little effort in this area usually produces large dividends.

INTERROGATING YOUR PARTNER			
Are you aware of doing this ?			
PARTNER A		PARTNER B	
YES	NO	YES	NO
☐	☐	☐	☐

31

7. THREATENING

- "I'm warning you. If you do that again, I'm leaving."

- "I'm going to hit you if you keep provoking me."

- "Do it once more and you can forget about sex."

- "I'm going to report you to the IRS."

- "I'm going to tell the children what you have been doing to me."

The basic message in this trap is that if you do something I don't like, or you fail to do what I want, I will threaten to retaliate.

If sometimes you need to protect yourself from your partner's hurtful actions, state your feelings and explain how you intend to act in the future. A calm and rational tone and style are enormously important. You can say, "It is terribly upsetting to me when you come home intoxicated. I know you enjoy drinking with your friends, but it's very difficult for me. I've decided that when it happens in the future, I will stay overnight at a friend's house until you sober up."

Remember, threats are aggressive; self-protection is assertive.

THREATENING

Are you aware of doing this ?

PARTNER A		PARTNER B	
YES	NO	YES	NO
☐	☐	☐	☐

8. TAKING CREDIT

When you make a good decision or do something clever, do you go out of your way to see that everyone knows about it, so that you can get the credit? Or, worse, do you take the credit when your partner deserves it? Or, do you allow others to praise you when it was your partner who had the brilliant idea? This is one situation when it is truly better to give than to receive.

Taking credit at work may be appropriately assertive and practical, but in close relationships it is harmful, unless you also give ample credit to your mate. It creates better feelings when you go out of your way to *give* credit to your partner, in private and in public: "That great idea was yours, honey," or, "I couldn't have done it without you," or, if you are talking to someone else, "Mary thought of it first."

Pam worked to support Tom through law school and spent many nights and weekends helping him with his assignments. After joining a prestigious law firm, he basked in the praise he received from his colleagues, family and neighbors without ever acknowledging Pam's contributions to his success. He couldn't understand when she finally filed for a divorce why she wanted half of the monetary value of his law practice.

TAKING CREDIT
Are you aware of doing this?

PARTNER A		PARTNER B	
YES	NO	YES	NO
☐	☐	☐	☐

9. BEING RIGHT

The desire to be right and the attempt to prove it are among the principal weapons in a competitive couple's battle of the egos. Sometimes this behavior is designed simply to gain approval and praise from your partner ("See how smart I am?"), but often it is used to demonstrate superiority. If you and your partner are adversaries instead of collaborators, you probably correct and contradict each other and defend your own position to the death, rather than exchange ideas and feelings.

Betty: "I gave you the information."
Don: "No, you didn't."
Betty: "I certainly did."

In an intimate relationship it is not important to be right, unless you're dealing with major decisions, such as, "Should our child have heart surgery or not?" In some cases, the issue is far less serious but the outcome is still of some importance. "Do we take the left turn or the right turn to get to the movie theater?" If you take the wrong turn, you may miss the beginning of the show.

There are clearly issues in which one person is right and the other is wrong. However, the *need* to be right and the attempt to demonstrate that you were right are ruinous. Any statement that involves "I'm right, you're wrong" or "I told you so" creates distance. I would almost go so far as to say that *when you're right, you're wrong* and *when you're wrong, you're right*. When you are right, your partner is compromised and the relationship may be harmed. When you're wrong, at least you have a chance to strengthen the relationship by acknowledging your error. Every time you point out to your partner that you were right and she/he was wrong, you're bringing her/him down. In relationships, it is certainly better to be wrong and acknowledge it than be right and boast about it. If you are factually correct, it is even *more* important to support your partner. "I think I'm right in this instance but often you're right. In any case, it's not that important."

Some people just wait for their partners to make a mistake and then they gloat, a maneuver that one patient of mine called "the gotcha phenomenon."

It takes a lot of psychological savvy to say, "I might be mistaken," "I could have misspoken," or "I may have misunderstood"; and it takes a strong ego and a lot of integrity to say "I don't know," "I was wrong," and "I'm sorry." While some people are overly modest and self-effacing, too many others need practice in saying these simple sentences.

In my opinion, **it is much better to be happy than to be right, and the two usually don't exist together, particularly on the home front.**

BEING RIGHT
Are you aware of doing this ?

PARTNER A		PARTNER B	
YES	NO	YES	NO
☐	☐	☐	☐

10. REGRETTING

"If things had only been different..." One often hears such statements as, "If I hadn't lost my job..." "If we had stayed in Cleveland..." "If Joey hadn't gotten sick..." "If we had only bought that house, we could have been happy."

Take whatever action you can to make things better, or else accept them as they are, but don't corrode your relationship by regretting the way things turned out. You make countless choices in life. Instead of brooding about what you should have done, focus on the benefits of the choice you made, figure out what you can do to improve your life *now*— and you will be much happier. Regretting serves no useful purpose. This trap is another reminder that **The Past Is Dead —We Live In The Present And Plan For The Future.**

REGRETTING			
Are you aware of doing this ?			
PARTNER A		PARTNER B	
YES	NO	YES	NO
☐	☐	☐	☐

11. UNIVERSALIZING YOUR OWN OPINION

"My way is the right way." "My opinion is the only reasonable one." Few of us make such absolute judgments directly. But there are many examples of this relationship trap in everyday life.

"Asparagus is delicious" is very different from "I love asparagus." Asparagus isn't good or bad; some people like it and some people loathe it. If you assume that your own opinion is the truth or that your taste is the standard of excellence, you are setting the stage for problems with anyone who disagrees with you. "That movie was awful," implies that anyone who liked it is a nitwit. Note the difference between the following statements:

A) "I didn't like the book but Maude loved it." (good)

B) "That book was trash but Maude loved it. " (poor)

Sometimes the language is even more intolerant, arrogant and insulting: "Anyone with half a brain could see that Smith would be a better president than Jones." Too bad for your relationship if your partner happens to prefer Jones.

The words *should* and *ought* are prime vehicles for this trap:

- "Women *should* have children."

- "You *ought to* get a second job because a normal husband supports his family."

Frank likes pornographic movies and magazines. Beth tells him "That's disgusting!" She always has the option of leaving him if she hates what he does so much. But, less drastically, she can ignore his porn watching, she can learn to enjoy it herself, or she can try in a rational and pleasant way to get him to do it less often. "That's disgusting" serves no purpose in a relationship except to drive your partner away.

Cultivate the habit of saying "I prefer.." "In my opinion..." "I believe..." "I may be mistaken but..." "It's my impression that..." "As I recall it..." and "It was right *for me*."

```
+-------------------------------------------------+
|            UNIVERSALIZING YOUR                  |
|               OWN OPINION                       |
+-------------------------------------------------+
|                                                 |
|          Are you aware of doing this ?          |
|                                                 |
|       PARTNER A          PARTNER B              |
|       YES   NO           YES   NO               |
|        □     □            □     □               |
|                                                 |
+-------------------------------------------------+
```

12. CONFUSING THE PERSON WITH THE DEED

This trap involves making a general statement about a person when you are really talking about a particular quality or deed. For example, "Jim is inconsiderate" attacks Jim as a person, implying that being inconsiderate is his basic nature. "Jim did an inconsiderate thing by leaving without me" attacks the deed and not the person. It is better to say "*I thought* it was inconsiderate of Jim to leave without me," and still better to say "I wish Jim had waited for me."

"You are stupid" is extremely destructive, whereas "That was a stupid thing you did" is slightly less so. At least you are not indicting the whole person. It is more constructive to say, "I was upset when you spilled the paint." "I didn't like it when Lorraine put me down at the party" is better than "Lorraine is a bitch." Even your worst enemy has some redeeming qualities, and surely your partner has.

CONFUSING THE PERSON WITH THE DEED

Are you aware of doing this ?

PARTNER A   PARTNER B

YES   NO   YES   NO

☐   ☐   ☐   ☐

---

13. USING A DOUBLE STANDARD

Do you hold your partner to a stricter standard than you apply to yourself? "I am outraged if you keep me waiting, but it's all right if I'm late." "It's O.K. if I flirt but not if you do it." "You should be understanding if I have an occasional affair, but see how crazy I'll get if you try it." "If I leave a dish on the kitchen counter that's fine, but if you do it, God help you." "If my parents barge in on us without phoning first, it's not a problem, but with your family it's different."

Do you think it is all right for your partner to walk or take the bus so that you can have the car? And is it fine to buy what you like but unaffordable when your partner wants something of equivalent cost? Do you downgrade the importance of your partner's medical symptoms while exaggerating the significance of your own?

Jack always felt that his work (writing) was much more important than Thelma's interior decorating, even though she earned more than he did. In fact, he thought all of his activities were more important than hers. He frequently interrupted whatever she was doing to have her read changes in his manuscripts, but would become enraged if she ever interrupted him. He insisted that she ponder every word of every revision, however minor. One time she went to the doctor because of severe menstrual bleeding. The minute she returned, he asked if she had read his latest chapter.

Make yourself aware of the double standards in your relationship, and remember, a sound partnership depends on fair play.

USING A DOUBLE STANDARD
Are you aware of doing this ?

PARTNER A		PARTNER B	
YES	NO	YES	NO
☐	☐	☐	☐

14. DISPLAYING NEGATIVE DRAMATIC BEHAVIOR

A rich emotional life is part of a good relationship. Even the strong expression of negative feelings at times can be beneficial. However, negative drama (e.g., temper outbursts, tearful pleading) tends to create turmoil and makes your partner feel oppressed, manipulated and abused.

In my office work with couples, I stop anyone who uses negative dramatics. The reason is that patients come to me to help them solve problems, not for emotional catharsis. While an emotional release may help you feel better for the moment, the more emotional you are, the less clearly you are able to think. It is not only possible but necessary to learn how to communicate calmly in order to get along better with your partner. Several exercises in Part Three are specifically designed for this purpose.

As mentioned earlier, temperament to some extent has a biological basis, and people who have frequent disruptive emotional outbursts should seek psychiatric consultation. Certain antidepressants, other drugs designed to relieve anxiety, or medications that inhibit wide swings of mood, can be enormously helpful in some cases.

DISPLAYING NEGATIVE DRAMATIC BEHAVIOR

Are you aware of doing this ?

PARTNER A		PARTNER B	
YES	NO	YES	NO
☐	☐	☐	☐

15. USING NEGATIVE EMOTIONAL LANGUAGE

It is important to know the difference between *descriptive* language and *emotional* language. In the heat of passion, particularly when talking about yourself or your partner, do you tend to exaggerate or overdramatize? Using emotional language to express *positive* feelings enriches a relationship. Using Negative Emotional Language, especially in describing your partner's behavior, hurts the relationship. To eliminate negative undercurrents, you need to convert negative emotional language into descriptive language. Descriptive language gives a simple, emotionally uncharged statement about an event or person.

Sally made dinner for the family every night. One day Steve came home and found a note saying that she went to a lecture with a friend and would be home by nine. The note asked him to make dinner for himself and their daughter. When the couple came to see me, Steve described what happened this way:

Steve: "She *abandoned* the family; she walked out on us." (emotional)

Me: "You mean she went out one evening and asked you to make dinner for yourself and your daughter." (descriptive)

Hank and Ellen had a fight. Ellen left the house and

went to her parents' place for a few hours to calm down.

Hank: "When we have the slightest problem, the first thing she does is *run* to her mother."

Me: "You mean, last night she left for a couple of hours and went to her parents' place."

Barbara: "He jumps into bed with every floozy in town."

Me: "You mean last month when you were away, he had sex with another woman."

Jane: "When he didn't come to my mother's funeral because his business trip was more important, it left very deep scars."

Me: "You mean you felt hurt when he didn't come to your mother's funeral."

Watch out for negative emotional language. When dealing with negative feelings, practice using descriptive language instead. It will have a much better effect.

USING NEGATIVE EMOTIONAL LANGUAGE
Are you aware of doing this ?

PARTNER A		PARTNER B	
YES	NO	YES	NO
☐	☐	☐	☐

16. USING VAGUE TERMS

Using vague language, especially if it is negative, drives people farther apart. John says to Mary, "I want a woman who is nurturing," but a communications scientist would say, "I want a woman who is nurturing, and by nurturing I mean rubbing my back every night, saying you love me at least once a day, bringing me chicken soup in bed when I am sick, telling me that I am intelligent, witty, generous, charming and sexy, and not disagreeing with me in public."

If your relationship is fine, it's not necessary to be scientific. On the other hand, if things are not going well, it is essential to learn better ways of communicating. It is helpful to define words like "mean," "vicious," "crazy," and "unscrupulous," as well as positive terms like "normal," "loving" and "good husband" when they are used negatively, as in the "nurturing" example above.

Don't use vague negative terms. Make every effort to say exactly what you want, what you feel and what you mean. If you find yourself saying, "You aren't meeting my needs," or, "I'd like to have a normal life," or, "This is a sick relationship," or, "I want a commitment," tell your partner exactly what you mean by "meeting my needs," "a normal life," "a sick relationship," and "commitment."

USING VAGUE TERMS

Are you aware of doing this ?

PARTNER A		PARTNER B	
YES	NO	YES	NO
☐	☐	☐	☐

17. TAKING MEANINGLESS ISSUES SERIOUSLY

If you have ever seen a Woody Allen movie, you may recall that heavy psychological, philosophical or cultural discussions are among his main targets for ridicule. Discussions about existential despair, ontological anxiety and other abstract and arcane themes have a place in philosophy seminars, but usually not in domestic relations.

Questions and statements like the following often lead to confusion rather than clarity: "I need to figure out who I am," "Do you think we have a relationship?" "Where is our relationship going?" "Does our relationship have any meaning?" or, "Will we be together forever?" As in Using Vague Terms, it is much better to say what you want and what you think, or ask a specific question of your partner. Examples are "I love you," "I care about you, and I hope you feel the same way about me," "I hope we're happy together for a long time." "Do you think we're communicating?" is meaningless (in my opinion) whereas the specific question "What can we do to improve our communication?" is more practical.

I have seen many relationships in which Taking Meaningless Issues Seriously leads to stagnation, stalemate or turmoil without any enlightenment or change. Discuss real problems, especially if your relationship is not going well, and leave the abstract stuff to philosophers—and comedians.

TAKING MEANINGLESS
ISSUES SERIOUSLY

Are you aware of doing this ?

PARTNER A   PARTNER B

YES   NO   YES   NO

☐   ☐   ☐   ☐

18. USING PSYCHOLOGICAL WARFARE

This trap involves using psychological concepts and terms against your partner. Psychological warfare may take the form of labeling your partner as disturbed or neurotic, or asking a negative rhetorical question such as, "What's wrong with you?" If you have taken psychology courses, read books on the subject or had therapy, you are probably very skilled at this tactic. Therapists tend to be the worst offenders, in or out of the office.

The major weapons of psychological warfare are *labeling* and *interpreting*. Labeling might take the following form: "You're not normal, you're very childish, you're terribly immature, you're neurotic, you're sick, you're paranoid, you're a borderline psychotic with psychopathic tendencies." Even the more modest statement, "Your *behavior* is bizarre, abnormal, etc." is not much better. Some people, instead of saying, "you are," use the gentler "you have..." For example, "You have deep seated problems" or, "You have a very fragile ego." Others prefer the "you need" form: "You need help" or, "You need a mother."

The fullest creative possibilities for psychological warfare are found in the *interpretation*. Here the aggressive maneuver is couched in terms that seem to convey profound psychological insight. The notion of understanding causes of behavior comes into play, e.g., "You said that because you are basically insecure." or, "You're obviously afraid of intimacy and that's why you don't want to get married" or,

"It's clear that you have a lot of unconscious hostility toward women." The richer and more historical the explanation, the more convincing it tends to be: "The root of the problem is that you were not breast fed and therefore are desperately looking for a warm, nurturing mother figure." Or, "Your father was so seductive, how could you possibly have a normal relationship with a man?" It's bad enough to tell your partner what's wrong with him/her. Don't compound it by telling him "why." Enough therapists have made fools of themselves over the years with such statements as, "Your menstrual cramps are related to your ambivalence about being a woman," or, "Your inability to have an orgasm during intercourse means you are like a little girl who is afraid of being an adult," or, "Your chronic diarrhea is a manifestation of unconscious hostility."

My former habit of lateness was attributed during analysis to my mother's inordinately long labor when I was born. The analysis lasted much longer than the labor and was far less productive. There is an old wisecrack in psychiatric circles about adding insight to injury. DON'T!

USING PSYCHOLOGICAL WARFARE

Are you aware of doing this ?

PARTNER A   PARTNER B

YES   NO   YES   NO

☐   ☐   ☐   ☐

19. MAKING NEGATIVE COMPARISONS

There are several versions of this trap:

1) Comparing your partner to a detested or disreputable person: "You're just like your mother" or, "You're a real Hitler."

2) Comparing your partner unfavorably with an alleged superior: "You don't see Louie treating *his* wife that way." A variation of this assault is, "Why can't you be like Louie?"

3) Comparing your partner with yourself: "You don't see *me* doing that." "You don't see *me* yelling when *you're* late." "*I* wouldn't do a thing like that to *you*." While you may not do that particular thing to your partner, you probably do others that are equally irritating.

4) Comparing your partner with a hypothetical standard: "Why don't you act your age?" or, "Can't you act like a normal person?" When I was a teenager, my mother used to say to me, "Why can't you act like a human being instead of a wild animal?"

It is particularly dangerous to compare unequal situations. A spouse of 20 years and a lover of 3 months whom you see once a week are hardly comparable. Comparing your partner unfavorably to former lovers (not to mention current or future) is obviously most destructive.

MAKING NEGATIVE COMPARISONS

Are you aware of doing this ?

PARTNER A		PARTNER B	
YES	NO	YES	NO
☐	☐	☐	☐

---

20. SAYING "NO"

Saying "No" is considered one of the cornerstones of assertiveness. Yet in intimate relationships, it can be deadly. If your partner asks you for something and you say "no," the resulting damage will depend partly on how much your partner wants what he is asking for, how you say "no" and whether your partner takes it as a rejection of *him/her*.

The whole interplay of asking and responding is a critical part of the communication process. However you handle it, don't say "no." This doesn't mean that you must do everything your partner wants you to do. Total compliance would be impossible and absurd. It does mean making every effort to say "yes."

Some requests seem reasonable and others not. If you are the one who says "no" frequently, then next time your partner makes a request ask yourself the following questions:

1) Do I think it is reasonable?

2) Will it cause harm to me or others? Will it inconvenience me a great deal or interfere with other important or enjoyable activities?

3) Will it be good for the relationship? Will it promote affection and/or respect?

If you don't have a problem with the request after answering these questions, why not go ahead and do what your partner asks? However, if you have a good reason for declining, there are constructive ways of doing so. Here are some negative and positive examples:

A: "Honey, when you're downtown would you pick up a couple of magazines for me?"

B: 1) "No, I won't".

   2) "Do it yourself."

   3) "I'd rather not."

   4) "I can't."

   5) (Giving a reason) "I can't because I have to be back at 2 o'clock."

   6) (Starting with a positive) " I'd love to, but I can't because I have to be back at 2 o'clock."

   7) (Suggesting an alternative) " Can one of the kids get them for you when they come home from school?"

   8) (Combination of 5, 6 and 7) "I'd love to, but I have to be back at 2 o'clock and I don't think I'll have the time. Can one of the kids get them for you when they come home from school?"

Another Example:
A: "How about making love?"

B: 1) "I don't feel like it."

2) "Not now."

3) "I'd love to, but my sex drive isn't as strong as yours. How about if I satisfy you?"

4) "I'd love to, but I think I'm too tired to respond. How about my satisfying you?"

5) "I'd love to, but I'm exhausted. How about in the morning?"

A more subtle but still unhelpful way of saying "no" is the *conditional positive response:*

A: "Would you do me a favor?

B: 1) "That depends. What is it?" (Poor)

2) "What is it?" (Fair)

3) "Sure, what is it?" (Good)

If you say "Sure," and the request then seems unreasonable or unmanageable, you can always revise your answer and explain. Don't slam the door on your partner and your own happiness before you find out what's involved. Use the following steps:

1) Start with a positive response. ("Sure.")

2) Offer a non-rejecting explanation.

3) Suggest a specific alternative.

Example:
A: "Honey, would you do me a favor?"

B: "Sure, what is it?"

A: "Would you ask your brother if we could borrow money for the taxes we owe?"

B: "I know it would be a big help, but I'd feel too uncomfortable asking because we already owe him six thousand dollars. What about increasing the mortgage on our house?"

Years ago, there was a popular song entitled "Please Don't Say No, Say Maybe." In intimate relationships, do everything possible to say "yes"—not necessarily yes to every request, but a resounding yes to the relationship.

SAYING NO			
Are you aware of doing this ?			
PARTNER A		PARTNER B	
YES	NO	YES	NO
☐	☐	☐	☐

21. APPEALING TO OR QUOTING THIRD PARTIES FOR SUPPORT

Do you recall ever making this kind of statement to an outsider—friend, relative, therapist?

- "I ask you, is it so unreasonable? I come home from a hard day's work and all I want is a little peace and quiet. Is that so much to ask?"

- "Isn't it true that Lucy started the fight we had at the party?"

If you appeal to a third party to support your position, you've lost, no matter what answer you get. Either way, divisions are widened. When talking to your partner, invoking the names of third parties as authorities is a variation: "Even Dr. West said I was right. You can ask him" or, "Even your brother agreed with me." This trap is similar to Being Right. (Trap #9)

If you have a difference with your partner, resolve it between yourselves. If you do consult a third party, make sure that person brings you closer together, rather than drive you farther apart.

APPEALING TO THIRD PARTIES FOR SUPPORT

Are you aware of doing this ?

PARTNER A		PARTNER B	
YES	NO	YES	NO
☐	☐	☐	☐

22. BEING INATTENTIVE

Inattentiveness takes many forms including: not responding to what your partner says or does; not replying verbally; not looking at your partner; walking away from your partner when he/she is talking; turning away from your partner and talking to someone else; abruptly changing the subject; ignoring issues that are important to your partner; looking at other men or women when you are with your partner; and appearing preoccupied when your partner is with you.

Falling asleep when your partner is trying to communicate can also create problems. Sometimes there may be a biological reason for this habit (a specific sleep disorder requiring treatment, other medical problems or a medication side effect). In these cases, it is a good idea to tell your partner that you are interested in what he/she is saying, but add that you're feeling very sleepy.

Inattentiveness may take more active forms, such as frequent interrupting or monopolizing conversations. It is particularly difficult to observe yourself doing this, and you may want to ask others, including your partner, about your inattentiveness. Attentiveness is one of the secrets to a successful social life and domestic relationship.

BEING INATTENTIVE

Are you aware of doing this ?

PARTNER A		PARTNER B	
YES	NO	YES	NO
☐	☐	☐	☐

23. FAILING TO RESPOND POSITIVELY

When your partner does something you like, especially if it is new, better or more frequent, seize the opportunity to praise her/him for it. Sometimes one of my skeptical patients will say, "What am I supposed to do, give him a medal for walking the dog once a year?" If you want him to do it once a month, then once a week and eventually every day the answer is "Yes." This advice is based on the psychological principle called *reinforcement of successive approximations*, or *shaping*. Praise your partner for the 10 percent you get, and you're likely to get 20 percent, and then much more. If you wait to say anything positive until you get 90 or 100 percent, you're apt to wait a long time.

For the first time in a 15-year relationship, your partner ineptly attempts to make the bed. What is your response likely to be?

1) "Don't bother if that's the best you can do."
2) Ignore it.
3) "I appreciate your help."

Your partner prepares an excellent dinner—an hour late. What do you think you would say?

1) "How come dinner is so late?"
2) "This is a great meal."

One of the most dangerous failings in a relationship is taking the positives for granted. Some of us don't respond positively to our partners even if we get 100 per cent of what we want, but we are quick to pounce when dissatisfied. This orientation is guaranteed to wreck a relationship.

Praise isn't the only way to strengthen your partner's desirable behavior. Anything you say or do that pleases your partner can *reinforce* the behavior. Here's how it works:

1) Do or say the positive thing *at the time* your partner does something you like, rather than a day or a month later;

2) Support your partner in a way that is meaningful to him or her. Giving chocolate to an obese partner, or sending flowers to an allergic spouse will not have the desired effect.

Fred couldn't understand why Janet didn't shower him with affection after he bought her a fur coat. In my office he said, "What does she want? I gave her a fur coat, spent $5,000 on a trip to Europe and took her out for dinner almost every night." The answer to his question was "encouragement for my work, more hugging, and your coming home earlier at night." The dinners and European trip were mainly for him, and the fur coat wasn't that important to her. It is particularly sad and wasteful to make sacrifices in the mistaken belief that your partner benefits from what you are doing.

A relationship has to be nurtured, and praise (positive reinforcement) is the cornerstone of this process. Don't leave your happiness to chance. Take the opportunity to influence your partner's behavior in a way that will make your life better—by supporting the positives.

FAILING TO RESPOND POSITIVELY

Are you aware of doing this ?

PARTNER A		PARTNER B	
YES	NO	YES	NO
☐	☐	☐	☐

---

24. INVALIDATING PARTNER'S PERCEPTION

Do you frequently fail to validate your partner's perceptions, impressions, interpretations, and recollections? Fred and Nancy were returning home from a party and Fred said, "Wasn't it shocking when Midge said she was divorcing Dick?" Nancy replied blandly, "Did she say that? What's so shocking about it?" If Nancy were in the habit of validating Fred, she might have said, "Yes, it was surprising" or, "I must have missed it, but it is shocking" or, "It's not all that surprising, because, if you remember, a few weeks ago she dropped a hint about it" or, "I heard something like that but I thought what she meant was that she had considered leaving Dick but then changed her mind."

The issue is not whether you agree or disagree with your partner's statement, nor whether you recall an experience the way he/she does. Nor should you say "yes" to your partner every time he opens his mouth. The point is to establish contact, be as close and supportive as possible, and have a give-and-take dialogue rather than shut your partner out.

Another way of invalidating your partner's perception is to dampen his/her enthusiasm by saying things like, "I don't think that's particularly amusing" or, "There's nothing new about that, I heard it years ago" or, "I don't think it's so important." Invalidating your partner in public is even worse.

The most malicious form of this trap is called "gas lighting" (from the famous 1944 movie with Ingrid Bergman and Charles Boyer), deliberately creating incidents that will upset your partner and then denying that they ever happened.

INVALIDATING PARTNER'S PERCEPTION	
Are you aware of doing this ?	
PARTNER A	PARTNER B
YES NO	YES NO
☐ ☐	☐ ☐

25. PUNISHING THE POSITIVE

This trap occurs when your partner does or says something nice and is punished for it. The punishment often involves contradiction or criticism. My mother, who loved her family more than her own life, would nevertheless respond to a Mother's Day gift of flowers by saying, "What good are flowers? They're very expensive and die in a few days. You shouldn't have wasted the money." Some cynics are fond of quipping, "No good deed goes unpunished."

Failure to praise your partner's desirable qualities (Trap #23) is one way of damaging feelings, but punishing positive behavior is worse. One common method of Punishing The Positive is to say something supportive but spike it with a hostile qualifier:

- "Thanks for doing the dishes. I thought I'd never live to see it."

- "That's the first nice thing you've said to me in twenty years."

- "That was a good investment you made; it's too bad you've had so many losers."

There are many ways of responding to your partner's positive words and deeds. As discussed under Trap #23, saying or doing something nice in return is usually best, but there are different degrees of positive response. A neutral or mildly positive response can easily be interpreted as punishment by your partner.

Suppose your partner says, "You are wonderful (sexy, brilliant ...)." What are you apt to say?

1) "You don't know what you're talking about." (Assault)

2) "I am not." (Contradiction—maybe hostile or just modest)

3) "I have to put the kids to bed." (Change of subject because of indifference or embarrassment)

4) (Say nothing—no response)

5) "I know." (Self-centered)

6) "Thank you." (Positive acknowledgement)

7) "You are pretty wonderful yourself." (Supportive and reciprocating)

8) "I love it when you say things like that to me." (Positive coupling)

Isn't it clear that consistent use of the last two or three responses will enrich most relationships? In a similar vein, there are many ways of reacting to a shared positive experience, such as a movie, dining out, sex, or a vacation:

1) Negative comments about the experience or about your partner: "It was okay, but not great," "You spoiled it with your gum chewing," "Why couldn't you have done this ten years ago?"

   Partner A: "I'm sorry you didn't enjoy it."
   Partner B: "You should be sorry."

2) Saying nothing.

3) Positive but impersonal or non-personal: *"That* was nice" or, "That's what I call good sex" or, "The Grand Canyon is beautiful."

4) Positive but self-centered: "I had a good time" or, "I love Italian food" or, "I had three orgasms."

5) Supportive: "You picked a great show" or, "You are a wonderful lover."

6) Coupling response: "The Grand Canyon was great, but the best part was being together" or, "Life with you is wonderful" or "I love you."

Do you know which of these patterns you use most often? There is nothing wrong with 2, 3 and 4, but if you want a better relationship, try adding more 5's and 6's to your repertoire. Isn't it clear that "I miss you" is more personal and intimate than "I'm lonely"?

To sum up, when your partner does something positive, or you have a pleasant experience together, omit the poison darts and the zingers and be sure to be as positive as you can in return.

PUNISHING THE POSITIVE

Are you aware of doing this ?

PARTNER A		PARTNER B	
YES	NO	YES	NO
☐	☐	☐	☐

---

26. DOING A GOOD DEED, SOURLY

Did you ever do something to please your partner and then wonder why it wasn't appreciated? In this trap, you do something nice, but make it clear that you resent doing it, thereby ruining the experience for your partner.

Sue: "I'd like to invite my brother for dinner this week."

Mike: "All right, if you must, but it'll be just one more wasted night."

It is fine to say "Honey, this is a bad week for me, could we do it next week?" or, "Great, but I've got a ton of work to do. Would it be okay if I excuse myself for a couple of hours after dinner?"

The point is that if you decide to do something for your partner, do it with a smile or don't do it at all. If your partner thinks that you are really enjoying the experience when you aren't, he/she doesn't know you very well, and you can correct the erroneous notion another time.

Too many of us give with one hand and take away with the other. We ruin it not only for our partners but for ourselves.

DOING A GOOD DEED, SOURLY

Are you aware of doing this ?

PARTNER A   PARTNER B

YES   NO   YES   NO

☐   ☐   ☐   ☐

27. DEVALUING PARTNER'S CONTRIBUTIONS OR ACCOMPLISHMENTS

- "So you have a Ph.D., what's so great about that? It doesn't pay the rent."

- "You don't do anything but cook and take care of the kids. You should get some experience in the *real* world."

- "All those piano lessons—where did they get you?"

Taking your partner's desirable qualities for granted is bad enough, but actively devaluing them is far more destructive.

Some years ago, at a party, I was chatting with a friend of the family, a brilliant and charismatic scholar, when someone nearby mentioned with great admiration that his wife spoke French fluently. The scholar promptly told me, within the hearing of others, that learning a foreign language is meaningless, since one language was adequate for expressing one's ideas. Although this narcissistic and grandiose man had received numerous accolades for his work, he had almost no capacity for friendship and love, and was a bitter and unhappy human being.

Your partner undoubtedly makes contributions to your welfare and the well being of your family, and she/he surely has some worthwhile achievements and accomplishments. Support these contributions and accomplishments whenever possible, even if they are not in areas you particularly understand or enjoy. Above all, don't devalue them.

DEVALUING PARTNER'S CONTRIBUTIONS OR ACCOMPLISHMENTS

Are you aware of doing this ?

PARTNER A		PARTNER B	
YES	NO	YES	NO
☐	☐	☐	☐

---

28. DEMANDING PURE MOTIVES

- "You say nice things because you know it pleases me, not because you really mean them."

- "You have sex just to satisfy me, not because you really want to."

The fact is that you never know with certainty whether your partner "really" loves you or doesn't, or "really" wants to do something or doesn't. You are not able to read minds. All you know is what your partner says and does—her/his verbal statements and actions. While it is much better if your partner's behavior *and* feelings are positive, good treatment is always better than rotten treatment, regardless of the motives. I personally would rather be treated magnificently by a woman who didn't love me than abominably by a woman who did.

When you are working together to make things better, you may think, "It doesn't mean anything if it's not spontaneous." New skills are rarely "spontaneous." Americans don't speak fluent Japanese spontaneously without *lots* of practice. Nor do piano playing, tennis or communication skills become spontaneous until they are practiced. As you know, behavior change often leads to feeling change.

In some ways it means *more* if your partner does something because it pleases you. His/her willingness to work at

the relationship may be more valuable than the fact that both
of you just happen to like baseball or ballet.

DEMANDING PURE MOTIVES

Are you aware of doing this ?

PARTNER A		PARTNER B	
YES	NO	YES	NO
☐	☐	☐	☐

---

29. USING "ALWAYS" AND "NEVER"

- "We never go out anymore."

- "We always make love the same way."

- "Every time I ask you a question you ignore me."

Do these sound familiar? If you are going to make a negative comment, it's a little better to say:

- "We haven't been going out *much* these days."

- "We *usually* make love in the same position."

- "*Often*, when I ask a question, you don't answer."

A *request* for what you want is even better than your negative comments:

- "Would it be all right with you if we went out more often?"

- "Let's get one of those sexy shower gadgets for the next time we make love."

- "I really value your opinion and would like to know what you think of this."

If you catch yourself saying things like, "You've never said a kind word to me," "You're always late," "You never do anything with the children," practice substituting *often, sometimes, frequently, rarely*, and *seldom*.

USING ALWAYS AND NEVER

Are you aware of doing this ?

PARTNER A		PARTNER B	
YES	NO	YES	NO
☐	☐	☐	☐

---

30. EXTRACTING REASSURANCE

- "Do you love me?
- "Tell me you're not seeing anybody else."
- "Do you think I'm a failure?"
- "Do you find me attractive?"
- "Do you think I'm bright?"

While it is delightful to hear positive things from your partner, it is debilitating when you have to extract the sentiments from him/her. Besides, what you get under duress isn't worth much.

There is certainly nothing wrong with asking, "Do I look nice tonight?" It is even reasonable on occasion to prompt your partner with, "I really like it when you tell me I'm a great cook." But repeated requests for reassurance do not promote closeness; in fact, they do just the opposite. This theme runs throughout relationships:

When you are feeling frustrated, needy or desperate, your actions will often produce exactly the opposite result from the one that you want.

EXTRACTING REASSURANCE

Are you aware of doing this ?

PARTNER A		PARTNER B	
YES	NO	YES	NO
☐	☐	☐	☐

31. EXTRACTING COMMITMENTS

In many circles, it is considered a sign of maturity to make commitments, and a sign of immaturity not to make commitments. Some commitments have ethical and legal implications, but most don't. Many are made under duress and others are appropriate only to formal contracts.

People's feelings change and circumstances change. While there have to be basic understandings and agreements for day to day continuity as well as for future planning, pressing your partner for commitments often creates a coercive atmosphere and leads to resentment. Most importantly, don't extract commitments if what you are requesting is vague or unenforceable. If you ask your mate to agree to do the dishes or walk the dog half the time, that's specific and practical. But "I want you to promise you will never get drunk again" or, "Tell me you'll never leave me" can cause serious problems. Such promises are usually not realistic, specific enough or enforceable.

In short, if you pressure your partner to do something she/he doesn't want to do or would have great difficulty doing, particularly if a long-term commitment is involved, you may get appeased and reassured for the moment, but you're setting the stage for future resentment and broken promises.

EXTRACTING COMMITMENTS

Are you aware of doing this ?

PARTNER A   PARTNER B

YES   NO   YES   NO

☐   ☐   ☐   ☐

32. GIVING ADVICE WITHOUT BEING ASKED

Telling your partner what's right or wrong, what she should do, or what's good for him, especially if you invade his territory without being asked, can be very irritating.

Leo expects Elaine to do the cooking, and she is willing, but he cannot resist advising her to add more salt or use less butter, and reminding her that the roast will be overdone if she cooks it any longer. He is shocked when, one day, she dumps the stew on his head and storms out of the house.

Penny is a bug on health and bombards Al with admonitions about the need for exercise, optimal nutrition and frequent medical appointments. She also delivers sermons on the toxicity of everything he eats, drinks and inhales. She cannot understand why the more she preaches the less he listens.

Martha is the classical backseat driver. When Todd is at the wheel, she demonstrates her reading proficiency by calling out most of the road signs, and she provides reports about pedestrian, motorist, and cyclist movements, as well as weather bulletins and reminders about when to slow down, pass or turn. After six years years of marriage, is it a wonder that Todd finally refuses to drive when they go out together?

If you are bursting with brilliant advice for your partner, it is better to say, "May I make a suggestion?" or, "I have an idea that might be useful." Even so, don't make a habit of giving gratuitous advice, especially in areas where your partner knows more than you do. One of my relatives, who has perfected this annoying habit, wouldn't hesitate for a moment to tell the head of IBM how to run the company.

Unsolicited advice is particularly irritating when it has a coercive, moralizing or critical tone. *Should* and *ought* are major culprits. "You should tell him that you don't want to do it" is not as constructive as "I think it might be a good idea to tell him you can't do it."

**GIVING ADVICE
WITHOUT BEING ASKED**

Are you aware of doing this?

PARTNER A   PARTNER B

YES   NO   YES   NO

☐   ☐   ☐   ☐

---

33. GIVING ORDERS

Do you sometimes act like a Marine sergeant with your partner, giving orders and barking commands?

- "Don't go into my closet!"
- "Turn off the TV!"
- "Get off the phone!"

"Don't touch me there!" is not as endearing as, "It feels better when you touch me here." "Stop shouting!" is not the same as "Please speak a little more softly."

The worst examples are reminders that your partner violated your order.

- "I told you not to bring any more beer into this house!"

- "Didn't I tell you to shut the refrigerator door?"

When we were kids we were taught to say "please" and "thank you." A few of these old teachings have great value. Asking is better than telling, and a request is much better than an order.

GIVING ORDERS

Are you aware of doing this ?

PARTNER A		PARTNER B	
YES	NO	YES	NO
☐	☐	☐	☐

34. ABUSING A CONFIDENCE

Partners usually share personal feelings and sensitive information with each other. The sense of trust and the belief that you will not be betrayed are among the cornerstones of an intimate relationship. The capacity for self-disclosure is an important ingredient of mental health, but disclosing for others, especially without their consent, is another matter.

Do you have a loose tongue when it comes to confidences? When you are angry, do you ever bring up one of these sensitive topics or indiscreetly disclose personal details about your partner to others? Anyone can make a thoughtless slip, but if such slips become habitual, they can undermine a relationship. When they are willful and malicious the damage is incalculable.

Charlie was fired from his job and didn't want anybody except Judy to know about it. He was horrified to learn that Judy had told her parents, who in turn passed it along to their best friends and to Judy's sister.

If you feel you must reveal something intimate about your partner, make certain that the person you tell will not share it with others. Better yet, keep the information to yourself.

ABUSING A CONFIDENCE

Are you aware of doing this ?

PARTNER A		PARTNER B	
YES	NO	YES	NO
☐	☐	☐	☐

35. TALKING NEGATIVELY ABOUT YOUR PARTNER TO OTHERS

Speaking ill of your partner to others sows the seeds for your continued misery. If you have a problem with your partner, work it out with him or her. Tell him/her what's wrong and what you would like. However, the tensions that exist in every relationship do necessitate blowing off steam once in a while. Everyone needs to express feelings, and people who do so are better off than those who keep things bottled up. Most of us have one or two intimate friends who can be trusted with anything.

Make sure that if you speak ill of your mate to a friend, the friend has your best interest at heart. Jill confided to her friend Nancy that Ken hit her. From that day on, even though Jill and Ken made up, Nancy would not speak to Ken or even be in his presence. This reaction may be loyal, but a friend who loves you will respect your right to decide what's best for you rather than impose her standards on you. Several years ago I confided to a close friend something that distressed me about my wife. I subsequently learned that he disclosed this information to a third party who then related it to my wife. I believe that everyone needs a therapist, but it's important to pick your therapist carefully, whether it be a trained professional or the home grown variety.

TALKING NEGATIVELY ABOUT YOUR PARTNER TO OTHERS

Are you aware of doing this ?

PARTNER A		PARTNER B	
YES	NO	YES	NO
☐	☐	☐	☐

36. GETTING EVEN

If you feel wronged by your partner and are disappointed, upset, hurt or angry, do you retaliate? Do you think to yourself, "I'll show her/him"? Doing things for spite or vengeance demeans you and cripples your relationship. Your partner may have said or done something unfair and you may be entirely justified in being angry, but nobody benefits from your getting even.

April wants to make love but Sy turns her down because he is angry. She then refuses to have sex with him for the next few weeks. He retaliates by telling her that it doesn't matter because she's frigid anyway. Sy could have made love and at another time tried to resolve the problem. Or, if his negative feelings really interfered with his sexual desire, he could have said so in a constructive way and tried to work it out at the time. April's hurt feelings about being rejected could have been expressed in a better way. As bad as getting even is, using sex as a weapon is particularly destructive. Sy, instead of compounding the damage, could have explained that he had been upset and really did find April desirable. This example illustrates the kind of escalation that occurs when couples fall into the Getting Even trap.

If you feel you've been hurt, say so; if you feel wronged, say so; if you want some compensation from your partner, say so. If you want to take steps to protect yourself, do so;

and if you want to end the relationship, do that. But retaliation, vengeance and spite have no place in a wholesome partnership.

GETTING EVEN
Are you aware of doing this ?

PARTNER A		PARTNER B	
YES	NO	YES	NO
☐	☐	☐	☐

37. MAKING EXCUSES

- "I've been worried about my tax audit and that's why I forgot your birthday."

- "I had a bad session wiui the shrink, and I was too upset to do the bills."

- "The car broke down."

- "The boss kept me late."

If you agree to do something, do it. If you are not going to do it, say so as soon as you realize that the situation has changed. If you agreed to do something and for some reason didn't do it, apologize or make it up to your partner in some way. Whatever you do, Don't Make Excuses. Making excuses demeans your partner and you. Apologies are more apt to promote closeness than are excuses. Still, if you repeatedly renege on agreements, even apologies aren't worth much. Many people take moral pressure off themselves by apologizing, without changing their behavior in any way.

At times, there are reasonable explanations for inconveniencing your partner. People do occasionally get stuck in unforeseeable traffic jams, work situations, emergencies and the like. But repeatedly evading responsibilities or failing to live up to agreements damages relationships. Making excuses only adds to the problem.

MAKING EXCUSES

Are you aware of doing this ?

PARTNER A		PARTNER B	
YES	NO	YES	NO
☐	☐	☐	☐

38. LYING

Lying is universal. We probably couldn't survive without it, and, not all lies are malicious or exploitative. Many are harmless or even beneficial, such as lies to cover ignorance, to make life easier for other people, or to surprise someone you love. But lies that involve exploitation, over-protectiveness or concealment of wrongdoing are harmful and can spell trouble for a relationship.

Lying in an intimate relationship undermines the relationship. Even if your partner doesn't know about the lie and never finds out, the relationship will probably still be damaged. You have devalued your partner and will therefore have less respect for her/him and for yourself.

Gratuitous lying, that is, lying when you haven't been questioned by your partner, is particularly destructive. Active lies are usually more damaging than lies of omission. Some partners actually ask to be deceived rather than confront certain painful realities. "I don't care if you're having an affair, I just don't want to know about it." If you lie frequently, see if there are instances in which you can say, "I'd rather not discuss it." It is better to say nothing than to lie.

Make yourself aware of how much you lie, and don't allow yourself to do it automatically. This is not a plea to tell the truth all the time, but rather to lie as little as possible to your partner.

LYING

Are you aware of doing this ?

PARTNER A		PARTNER B	
YES	NO	YES	NO
☐	☐	☐	☐

39. COMPULSIVE TRUTH-TELLING

You may feel that it is important to be completely and totally open with your partner, disclosing and discussing all of your activities, and even your fantasies. There are few relationships that can tolerate this degree of sharing, and there is even something hostile about compulsive truth-telling, especially when the disclosures are upsetting. I have never been impressed by people who make belated "confessions" to their partners about activities the partner would deplore.

If five years ago you had a brief affair with someone and now have some psychological need to share the information, it is better done with a therapist or pastor. If the particular incident has had a major impact on your partner, it might be helpful to disclose it, apologize and make amends. Usually, though, what's done is done. If it was hurtful, *don't do it again*. If you are sharing upsetting news because you want your partner's help (e.g., someone addicted to drugs who "slips"), such sharing might be all right, provided your partner understands and is able to respond constructively.

Unexpected, unsolicited, unnecessary, intrusive and upsetting truth telling is deadly. If you have the impulse, resist it—even if your therapist or encounter group tells you otherwise.

COMPULSIVE TRUTH-TELLING

Are you aware of doing this ?

PARTNER A		PARTNER B	
YES	NO	YES	NO
☐	☐	☐	☐

40. BEING JEALOUS

Cindy and Bob have been together for four years. She loves him and shows it in many ways, but she is on the verge of leaving him because he gets furious when the phone rings and it is a wrong number, when any man converses with Cindy at a party, when she talks to her former husband, when she goes out with her friends, or when she comes home from work half an hour late. He has even gone through her handbag and dresser drawers on several occasions, supposedly looking for keys or change, but actually searching for evidence of infidelity.

Jealousy is a negative emotional reaction based on the belief that your partner is or might become involved with someone else. It makes little difference whether your partner is actually interested in or involved with another person, since jealousy is usually a reaction to beliefs rather than facts. There is an enormous difference between what is in the world and what is in our minds, between real harm and perceived harm. One of the basic tenets of modern therapy is the statement that *we are not upset by events but by our beliefs and our interpretations*. In addition, what is far more important than what goes on *outside* the relationship is what is happening *inside* the relationship. If your partner spends as much time with you as ever and treats you as well as ever, that's all you can know. Getting upset about speculations is a waste of time.

On the other hand, if your mate, as a result of being involved with someone else, is less available to you for companionship or sex, that is a real issue. If he/she brings home venereal disease or lice, that too is real. Then you have a decision to make. Either you end the relationship, negotiate a new contract for a different kind of relationship, have your partner compensate you in some way for the inconvenience, pain and deprivation—or forget about it. Getting overly upset, creating an emotional scene or acting hostilely will not promote your best interest, even when the issue is real. More often than not, the issue is *symbolic*, based on speculation. **Too many of us react to symbolic issues rather than to real issues, and we react emotionally instead of rationally.**

If you interrogate your partner to get at "the truth," there are only a few possible outcomes—and they are all bad:

1) She/he *is* involved with someone else and will deny it. This response demeans you, and you will never know if you're being lied to or not.

2) Your partner is not involved with anyone else and will say so. You still won't be sure if this is the truth, and doubts will persist. In addition, your questioning may irritate and offend your partner.

3) Your partner *is* involved with somebody and will tell you the truth, in which case you're likely to be upset.

However, if exclusiveness is so important to you that you would definitely leave if your partner were involved with others, then by all means hire a detective. If his/her investigation confirms your suspicions, move out. Otherwise, don't waste your time. **Getting upset is useless, whereas action that gets you what you want makes a lot more sense.**

Jealousy means a lack of trust in your partner and a lack of confidence in yourself. It is another example of an emotional reaction that is likely to bring about exactly the result you fear most.

BEING JEALOUS

Are you aware of doing this ?

PARTNER A		PARTNER B	
YES	NO	YES	NO
☐	☐	☐	☐

---

41. TAKING THE IRRATIONAL PERSONALLY

Irrationality is a part of life. It exists in every person and every relationship, including yours. We all do and say illogical, irrational and destructive things at times. Although it is dangerous to label your partner's behavior "irrational," there are times when you need to know how to react to your partner's upsetting moods and actions. What is irrational? Many of the errors in this section, especially those involving direct personal attacks and negative generalizations, are irrational. Usually it is not irrational to express your honest opinion about something.

Saying "You're disgusting" is irrational (see Trap #11). Even the more specific statement "It's disgusting when you pick your teeth" is irrational, because some people may not find it disgusting. They may not be enchanted by it, but they don't seem to mind. "I hate it when you pick your teeth," is not irrational, because it is an honest statement of a personal reaction. It certainly is not the most pleasant way of expressing the feeling, but it is rational.

Enormous emotional upheaval results from taking irrational actions and statements personally, especially when they don't cause real harm. Of course, it is better if your partner doesn't make irrational negative statements to begin with, but your refusal to react emotionally will be a powerful force for changing your partner's offensive behavior.

What is the alternative to taking irrational behavior personally? Treating it *clinically*. If you were a therapist, and your patient said that you were an incompetent, stupid, ugly, malicious liar, would you take it personally and react emotionally, or would you attempt to find out what your patient was upset about? Although you are not literally your partner's therapist, in some way you and your partner *are* therapists for each other and can benefit greatly from a calm, rational reaction to each other's emotional behavior. When your partner is out of control, you have an opportunity to help him/her and your relationship.

TAKING THE IRRATIONAL PERSONALLY

Are you aware of doing this ?

PARTNER A		PARTNER B	
YES	NO	YES	NO
☐	☐	☐	☐

42. FAILING TO ACCEPT RESPONSIBILITY FOR YOUR OWN FEELINGS

If you are upset about something your partner did, accept the fact that you don't *have to* get upset. Believe it or not, **you can control your feelings and your reactions, if it is important enough and you know how.**

Different people react differently to the same event. The event *triggers* a reaction, but doesn't *cause* your particular reaction.

If you want to handle a difficult relationship more effectively, it is necessary to control negative feelings. The first step in controlling them is to accept responsibility for them. Practice telling yourself:

1) "I don't have to get upset."

2) "I am allowing myself to get upset by interpreting this event negatively."

3) "In most of these situations no *real* harm is being done."

"You upset me" is very different from "I was upset when you said that." "Your mother ruined my day" is not as accurate as "I didn't enjoy Thanksgiving dinner because I found your mother's remarks unpleasant." Other people's actions may *elicit* our feelings but they aren't the sole cause.

It isn't necessary to get upset or have your day ruined because of what someone else said or did. If you believe a statement like "He made me feel ugly," then he has too much control over your emotional life. No one but yourself can *make you* feel ugly.

Although positive feelings are also under your control, it is usually not as important to take responsibility for them. You surely wouldn't mind if your partner said, "You make me feel sexy," even though "I feel sexy when I'm with you" is more accurate. If your partner starts treating you coolly and then you feel upset and unsexy, it is much better to think, "I upset myself" or, "I allowed myself to get upset" or, simply, "I was upset yesterday when you didn't want to make love" than to say "You upset me and made me feel unappealing."

FAILING TO ACCEPT RESPONSIBILITY FOR YOUR OWN FEELINGS

Are you aware of doing this?

PARTNER A		PARTNER B	
YES	NO	YES	NO
☐	☐	☐	☐

43. ATTACKING YOUR PARTNER'S BASIC RELATIONSHIPS

Attacking your partner's parents or brother or sister or best friend, close business associates or even former spouse will surely create problems and hurt your relationship. Be as pleasant as you can to these people, unless they are actively trying to harm your relationship with your mate *and are succeeding.* If they are trying and not succeeding, don't help them by putting pressure on your partner. Being pleasant doesn't mean spending your life entertaining them or visiting with them every weekend, but it is important not to undermine or attack them. You are a free agent and have a right to see them or not. How you assert that right is the issue.

If you don't care for your partner's family and friends, encourage her to do her own thing with them, and, if it is important to her that you join in, do it to please her, at least some of the time. Don't ruin the relationship with your mate because you dislike her sister.

Bud and Gail have been married for two years. Bud has always been close to his parents and his younger sister, Patty. His sister is moody, irritable, angry, and frustrated, partly because she is unmarried. In addition, she doesn't work and receives a great deal of financial support from Bud. She has frequent tantrums and makes no secret of her disapproval of Gail. When Bud and Gail had started dating, Patty tried to break up their relationship. Gail was furious at Patty and frequently berated Bud for catering to his sister and tolerating her outrageous behavior. What Gail failed to realize was:

1) Everyone comes to a relationship with baggage. Patty was Bud's baggage and Gail knew this when she got into the relationship.

2) What's important is not how Bud treats Patty, but how he treats *Gail*.

3) Bud is in the middle. If Gail understands the position he is in and supports him, he will feel closer to her and probably more distant from his sister.

4) If Gail limits her contact with Patty and reacts to her *clinically* instead of *personally*, her life will be much easier.

5) Even if she could drive a wedge between Bud and Patty, Bud would resent her.

6) There is probably someone else close to Bud, besides Gail, who can discuss Patty's behavior without Bud getting defensive. Consultation with a therapist may help Bud handle his sister more effectively.

ATTACKING YOUR PARTNER'S
BASIC RELATIONSHIPS

Are you aware of doing this ?

PARTNER A		PARTNER B	
YES	NO	YES	NO
☐	☐	☐	☐

44. BEING OVERPROTECTIVE

- "I know what's best for you."

- "Leave it to me, I'll take care of everything."

- "You don't have to know about these things."

- "Just sign here."

Some of us enjoy being looked after, and protected. We may even find comfort in having others make decisions for us. But more often than not, when you play the overprotective role, it demeans your partner and gives the impression that she/he is not capable of taking care of her/himself.

Sometimes one of you manages all of the finances or does all the driving or makes all the mechanical repairs in the house. This division of labor is practical, since each of you is surely better at certain things. Problems arise when you are overprotective and managerial, and your partner would like to be involved or know what's going on.

Lisa and Harvey both work, and, in addition, she has $25,000 from her late father's insurance. Harvey invests all of their combined savings and becomes indignant when Lisa asks for information. His attitude is that he is the expert and she should trust him.

The issue usually has nothing to do with trust, but with sharing and mutual respect. A dependent is a dependent, a ward is a ward, and a partner is a partner. If you have a tendency to be overprotective, make every effort to share the decision making and, where you are in charge of a particular area, explain as much as possible to your partner.

BEING OVERPROTECTIVE
Are you aware of doing this ?

PARTNER A		PARTNER B	
YES	NO	YES	NO
☐	☐	☐	☐

45. SPEAKING FOR YOUR PARTNER

Telling other people what your partner wants, thinks or likes when she is present can be distressing. Speaking for your partner when he is not present can create problems if you are not accurately stating his views.

Joan and Sarah are discussing where they and their spouses will have dinner. Joan suggests Italian food, which Sarah's husband doesn't like, but Sarah says, "Jim wouldn't mind." It's usually better to say, "I'll check with Jim and get back to you." Some partners are consistently on target when speaking for their mates. Many are not. Even if you are right, it may be better to let him speak for himself.

Sometimes, speaking for your partner is a putdown. "Don't give him a book; he'll never read it." I hear this kind of comment often in couple therapy when one partner says, "*I'm* willing to do what you suggest, but *she's* not interested." My response is "Let her speak for herself."

SPEAKING FOR YOUR PARTNER

Are you aware of doing this?

PARTNER A   PARTNER B

YES   NO   YES   NO

☐   ☐   ☐   ☐

---

46. MAKING UNILATERAL DECISIONS

You make hundreds of decisions every day. Many of them do not involve or affect your partner; for example, you decide to wear brown shoes instead of black or to have lunch with your supervisor rather than at your desk. However, many decisions that you make do affect your partner, sometimes in an adverse way.

Ron wanted to buy a stock and withdrew $10,000 from a joint bank account without telling Vickie. The stock went down shortly thereafter. Arthur and Pam went to look at cars and decided to buy a white Cutlass. A couple of days later, Arthur placed the order and chose the color blue because the white one they had seen in the showroom had been sold. He knew that Pam wanted a white car, yet failed to consult her. Elsie bought theater tickets even though she knew that Ted didn't care for plays. In each of these cases the partner who wasn't consulted felt understandably hurt.

In some cases you know what your partner wants and in other cases you don't. Sometimes your partner may allow you to make the decision or even urge you to do so. Sometimes people make unilateral decisions and don't tell their partners until the last possible minute. Trudy gets very upset when Ed has to go out of town on business. To avoid these emotional scenes, he waits until the last minute to tell her.

Your partner has a right to know about any decision you make that affects him or her and to know about it as soon as you know, unless he/she wants it otherwise.

Always inform your partner of any *major* changes you are going to make, even if they won't directly affect her. If the decision is yours to make, it is not necessary or desirable to ask permission, but it does promote positive feeling to inform and even consult.

Lou made arrangements with his brother to go to Atlantic City for the weekend. When Barbara found out, she said "We're not going and that's that." It would have been better if Lou had discussed it with Barbara *before* making the plans, and if Barbara had said "I'd love to go with you but I'm very uncomfortable in casinos. Is there some other place we could go?" This example illustrates the difference between an *adversarial* and a *collaborative* style.

MAKING UNILATERAL DECISIONS

Are you aware of doing this ?

PARTNER A		PARTNER B	
YES	NO	YES	NO
☐	☐	☐	☐

---

47. MAKING MALIGNANT INTERPRETATIONS

If your partner doesn't remember your anniversary, does it mean he is losing interest, does it mean that he was ill at work and couldn't get to the store to pick up your present, did he order something really nice that hasn't arrived yet, is he planning a surprise party the following weekend—*or did he simply forget?*

When I was in my early 20's, a blind date turned her head away from a good night kiss on the cheek at the end of the evening. Thinking she didn't like me, I never called her, and was shocked to learn a few months later from the relative who had given me her phone number that she was very disappointed I hadn't called. My malignant interpretation deprived me and my date of future encounters.

When a malignant interpretation affects your behavior toward your partner, try to *verify your interpretation* by asking if his/her action really meant what you thought it meant.

How well you get along with your partner has a lot to do with the assumptions you make about him or her. If she is irritable, you may think on the one hand "She's a bitch" or, "She's angry at me" or, "She hates me." On the other hand you may tell yourself, "She's tired" or, "She's not feeling well" or, "She's having a bad day." If your immediate interpretation is malignant, ask yourself *if any other expla-*

nations are possible. If they don't come to mind quickly, take a few minutes to think about it. If necessary, use pen and paper and write them down. For example, your partner may simply forget because he is not used to doing what you expect. He may not have acquired the desirable habit of complimenting or remembering birthdays and anniversaries.

If you use this strategy of *benign interpretation,* you won't feel cheated, your partner won't feel guilty, and both of you can focus your energies on creating a new and pleasing habit.

If you make *benign* assumptions about your partner's actions (or lack of actions), you will feel better and your relationship will be smoother. This does not mean that abuse should be explained away, but if you are going to make a malignant assumption, check its accuracy with your partner, so that ill will doesn't fester in your brain for too long.

There are then two basic steps in changing the habit of making malignant interpretations:

1) Think of several benign explanations. (He didn't hear me, she was upset about the kids.)

2) Check the negative explanation with your partner. (When you didn't call me at work, I thought you might be angry. Is anything the matter?)

Avoid malignant interpretations. Don't make life more difficult than it is.

MAKING MALIGNANT INTERPRETATIONS			
Are you aware of doing this ?			
PARTNER A		PARTNER B	
YES	NO	YES	NO
☐	☐	☐	☐

48. EXPLOITING YOUR PARTNER'S WEAKNESS

Do you sometimes hit your partner when he's down, has made a mistake, doesn't know something or is helpless? Or, do you fail to help him when he is in trouble?

Mort doesn't have much confidence in his sexual ability. When he has difficulty getting an erection, Harriet tells him that he doesn't satisfy her. She would do well to learn other ways of communicating: "It's not your problem—it's our problem and we'll work it out" or, "Performance is irrelevant, pleasure is what sex is all about and there are lots of ways of having pleasure." It would be helpful as well for her to explore the various ways of attaining sexual satisfaction (manual, oral, self stimulation, vibrator).

There are many ways one partner can exploit the other's weaknesses, and all of them are destructive to both partners and to the relationship. Emily is a wiz at math. Dan has gone back to school and is having trouble with algebra. She doesn't offer to help and when he asks, she finds excuses not to. At a party Fran cannot remember someone's name and asks Jerry. He knows but gets annoyed when she asks, and he doesn't tell her. Louise has started a small business without Sam's help. Orders are pouring in but she has a temporary cash flow problem and needs a few thousand dollars to tide her over. Sam, who earns more than $100,000 dollars a year, doesn't offer to help and secretly hopes that she doesn't make it. Phil, who is interested in self-improvement and is very receptive to constructive criticism, frequently says "nucular" instead of "nuclear" and makes a few other pronunciation errors. Judy, who is an English teacher, doesn't say anything, even though she knows Phil is job hunting and has to impress prospective employers.

One of the great values of having relationships is in pooling talents, resources and efforts for mutual benefit. Competitiveness and lack of support produce not only feelings of distance and alienation in your partner but missed opportunities for self-improvement as well.

EXPLOITING
YOUR PARTNER'S WEAKNESS

Are you aware of doing this ?

PARTNER A		PARTNER B	
YES	NO	YES	NO
☐	☐	☐	☐

---

49. COMPLAINING

Many people have said to me that one of the purposes of a relationship is to vent feelings and to air complaints. They believe that life is tough and that everybody needs a safe place to let it all hang out. While there is some truth to this, there are ways of reporting events and feelings without complaining. Complaining is a way of transmitting your own bad feelings that pressures your partner to feel guilty or responsible, to feel sorry for you, or to do something for you. It is an indirect way of reaching out that actually creates distance. My view is that a more important purpose of relationships is mutual enhancement and mutual support.

Of all the traps listed in this section, complaining can be one of the most corrosive. It generally falls into three categories:

1) Complaining about the outside world: "My job stinks, the bus was crowded and smelly, the heat is terrible, I can't stand it anymore."

2) Complaining about your partner (see Traps #2 and #3, Disapproving and Criticizing, as well as Trap #35, Talking Negatively About Your Partner To Others): "You overcooked the steak, you look like a slob whenever we visit my family."

3) Complaining about your own physical or psychological state. Many people are in the habit of reporting on their internal states, often in great detail: "I am constipated; my hemorrhoids are acting up; my hair is falling out; I have wrinkles; I'm nervous, depressed..."

Although reporting *good* things often enriches relationships, there are times when even here narcissistic excess takes over. More than one of my patients has had the habit of sharing such felicitous news as "Honey, I just had the most marvelous bowel movement," expecting their partner, who is not a professional nurse, to jump for joy.

This section is not meant to suggest that couples should spend all their time together simply exchanging pleasantries. Remember, there is a big difference between *complaining*, *reporting* events, and *requesting* advice and assistance. People often report the day's happenings without complaint. Requesting your partner's advice or reaction can be helpful: "What do you think I should do about my boss's screaming?" Such questions are all right, provided you don't monopolize all the talent in the family for your particular problem. Nor is there anything wrong with, "Honey, would you get me an aspirin and a glass of water? I have a headache."

For most couples, the tone of the evening is set by the homecoming greeting. If you start with a barrage of complaints, emotional distance is the likely result. It is almost always better to start with the good news.

125

COMPLAINING

Are you aware of doing this ?

PARTNER A		PARTNER B	
YES	NO	YES	NO
☐	☐	☐	☐

50. MAKING NEGATIVE PREDICTIONS

Have you ever said, "If it's good, it won't last" or, "If it's bad, it will never get better"? I have sometimes heard, "I know he's going to leave me" or, "I know she's just waiting to find some rich guy and take off with him." Occasionally, I am confronted with a contradiction when people come to my office for help and announce, "Therapy isn't going to do anything for this relationship; it's beyond hope."

It probably doesn't matter if you are pessimistic, provided you are definitely ending your relationship. But if you have chosen to remain in it and want to make it better, an *assertive positive expectation* is critical ("Where there's a will, there's a way," or, "I know that we will both work hard to make it better"). About 10 years ago I wrote a book with my friend and colleague, Arnold Lazarus, entitled *I Can If I Want To*. It was written for individuals rather than couples but stressed this positive orientation.

If you have

- the desire to improve your relationship

- a positive expectation

- the knowledge and tools to make it happen

IT WILL HAPPEN.

Or, to put it more assertively, *it* won't happen; *you will make it happen.* People who have positive expectations fare much better than those who make negative predictions, even if they are equally unhappy at the outset. The only thing that counts is what you want—and how to accomplish it. A pessimistic outlook has no place in this scheme. There is a self-fulfilling quality about negative predictions; that is, negative predictions are more likely to result in negative outcomes.

Some people who have a pessimistic outlook are suffering from depression and could benefit from professional help. But many of us make negative predictions about our partners or about our relationships as a matter of habit. Don't do it.

MAKING NEGATIVE PREDICTIONS
Are you aware of doing this ?

PARTNER A		PARTNER B	
YES	NO	YES	NO
☐	☐	☐	☐

51. PREVENTING PARTNER FROM DOING WHAT'S IMPORTANT TO HIM/HER

Joe likes to go bowling with his friends on Wednesday nights. Anne resents Joe's hobby, and, besides missing him, she feels that he prefers his friends to her. On the other hand, she takes a literature course Tuesday evenings and is not available on those nights to have dinner with Joe. He doesn't like the idea and puts pressure on her to miss classes.

In the best relationships partners encourage each other to do their own thing. When thinking about your partner's activities, it is important to recognize the difference between harmful deprivation and mild inconvenience. If your partner does his own thing in a way that is hurtful to you, that is different from his doing something you would rather he not do. It is necessary to take a stand when your partner clearly neglects a basic responsibility or agreement, and does so repeatedly. But it is much better for your relationship when your partner feels free to do what he/she loves to do and you actually *encourage* him/her to do it. In the best relationships partners are protective and supportive of each other's cherished activities.

Of course, doing your own thing can be carried to an extreme. Lewis watches football on television all day Sunday and every Monday night and, in addition, plays poker every Thursday night and works every other Saturday. Although this lifestyle is manageable for bachelors and even some couples, it is a major strain for Carla who feels chronically deprived. Mollie is a bridge fanatic who plays at a club Monday through Thursday nights and all day Saturday, whereas Wally is a homebody who is disappointed that he can't spend as much time with her as he'd like. If your partner's activity is a real hardship for you, attempt to negotiate some kind of compromise. But don't give him/her a lot of grief, and don't obstruct the pursuit of something really important to her/him.

PREVENTING PARTNER FROM DOING WHAT'S IMPORTANT TO HIM/HER

Are you aware of doing this ?

PARTNER A		PARTNER B	
YES	NO	YES	NO
☐	☐	☐	☐

---

52. MIND READING

We all mind read to some extent. You probably make assumptions and interpretations about what your partner's behavior means or what she wants, how he feels or what she plans to do. *Don't assume*, especially if it's negative. *Check* with her before getting upset or trampling on her rights and feelings.

There are two mind reading errors:

A) Reading your partner's mind:

- "You obviously can't stand me."

- "You didn't say anything so I thought you didn't want to go to the party."

- "I figured you weren't going to use the car so I let Tim have it."

B) Assuming your partner can read your mind:

- "I thought you knew I was upset."

- "I thought it was obvious that I wanted to make love."

- "You should have realized I had a class tonight."

There are enough real conflicts. Don't add unnecessary misunderstandings.

The rule is: When in doubt about what your partner thinks, feels, wants, or means, ask! And, when you expect your partner to know what you think, what you want, how you feel and what you mean, don't leave it to chance. Be assertive! Tell him/her.

MIND READING	
Are you aware of doing this ?	
PARTNER A	PARTNER B
YES NO	YES NO
☐ ☐	☐ ☐

53. ALLOWING OUTSIDE INTERFERENCE

Outside interference may be perpetrated by relatives, friends or business associates who either dictate the conditions under which you live or encroach on your time together. They may interfere with your quiet time, disrupt dinner, mar vacations, wreck entertainment plans or destroy your sex life. You have a life at home and a life outside the home. It may be necessary for economic reasons to spend considerable periods of time out of the home, far beyond the traditional 40 hour work week. Both quantity and quality of time together are important. However much or little time you spend with each other, don't let outsiders ruin it.

In many relationships, children are the major problem. In others, a business associate who calls about crucial deals or emergencies can disrupt time together. It doesn't matter if you are a doctor saving lives or a maintenance person responding to gas leaks. If the relationship with your partner is important and you work together, you will find a solution.

Sometimes intrusions are more acceptable to one partner than the other. If your partner is the culprit, don't intimidate, threaten or restrict him/her. Don't offer or accept excuses for disruptive events. In an assertive way, through negotiation, attempt to work out a satisfactory way of dealing with the problem. The saddest cases involve intrusions that neither party wants.

Make a list of all of the interferences you can think of

that spoil your time together. See how many of these you both want to do something about. Sometimes the solution is as simple as the purchase of an inexpensive telephone answering machine. This device enables you to monitor phone calls and take only those that cannot wait. It is remarkable how many couples do not have a lock on their bedroom door and yet complain about children barging in when they are trying to talk privately or make love. If you are on call for emergencies, arrange to have someone cover for you. Get a babysitter for a couple hours even when you are home. If you are the one who creates or allows the disruption, figure out a way of making it up to your partner. You have it within your power to keep the world from destroying your life together. Do *whatever* it takes to insure your happiness.

ALLOWING OUTSIDE INTERFERENCE

Are you aware of doing this ?

PARTNER A		PARTNER B	
YES	NO	YES	NO
☐	☐	☐	☐

---

54. PRETENDING TO WANT A BETTER RELATIONSHIP WHEN YOU DON'T

Some of us go through the motions of saying, "I want our relationship to be better," or we may dutifully go to a therapist or a marriage counsellor without really wanting things to be better. Self-deception in this area is the worst error of all.

Ask yourself if this trap applies to you. Strange as it may seem, there are people who don't want their relationship to be better, because it means they may have to do things they don't want to do or feel things they are afraid to feel. Some of us are uncomfortable with too much closeness or find frequent sex unpleasant. Others are so angry and resentful that they will never put aside old hurts.

Ask yourself the following questions, which I pose to many of my patients, "Is there anything my partner could do that would satisfy me. If he/she could undergo a brain transplant operation and now had a different personality, would I accept the fact that he/she had changed, and would I be willing to work in good faith to make the relationship better?"

It is particularly distressing to see one partner working hard to improve things when in fact nothing will make a difference because the other is unmotivated or locked into

135

the past. Again, be careful to ask this of *yourself* rather than answer it for your partner. Self-deception on this issue can lead to great pain and expense.

PRETENDING TO WANT A BETTER RELATIONSHIP WHEN YOU DON'T
Are you aware of doing this?

PARTNER A	PARTNER B
YES NO	YES NO
☐ ☐	☐ ☐

There you have it—the 54 Traps that can prevent you from *making it as a couple.* It is the story of millions of miserable individuals and couples. Did you recognize yourself in any of the chapters? Which ones? In order to derive the maximum benefit from Part Two, it is important to review the traps that most affect you and practice the suggested changes. Repetition is one of the best ways to learn.

Building on the techniques in this section of the book, Part Three will provide additional tools to improve your overall relationship, regardless of the particular traps that enmesh you and your partner.

Part Three:
Relationship Tools

INTRODUCTION

Making it as a Couple is not difficult—but there's a trick to it. The trick is to step back, take a good, hard, honest look at *yourself*, particularly at what you're thinking and what you're doing. If you've done that, you've done well. But if you still think it's up to your partner to change, think again—and reread Part Two. The key to this whole process is in realizing that you have the power to take control of your relationship. By changing what *you* think and what *you* do, you change the relationship.

It is easy to recommend that you stop doing destructive things and change the way you think, but how is this change accomplished? Most people who see what is wrong with their relationship don't know how to make it better. What is needed for this task are tools, for without these mechanisms of change, you are apt to fail no matter how much intelligence, awareness, and good will you have. This single fact accounts for more relationship unhappiness than any other. That is why Part Three will describe more tools to help achieve the level of quality you want in your relationship. You can't have too many tools, for these are the catalysts of change.

If you are fairly successful at being a couple, you probably have already devised some of your own ways of airing grievances, solving problems and limiting damage. And most likely you have developed these mechanisms automatically, without deliberate planning. On the other hand, if you are not doing too well in your relationship, you need to apply practical psychology to your life together. You have the capacity to do it—all you need to do is look at the way you think and act, and practice some exercises. To repeat what was said earlier, if you devoted a fraction of the time, effort and thought to your relationship problems that you devote to your work or recreational activities, your life together would improve remarkably.

The exercises you read about here will seem unnatural and contrived. You may think some of them are too gimmicky. When something is done in a new way, it isn't natural. It will be a little awkward, at least in the beginning. There is nothing sacred about being natural and spontaneous, especially if your relationship is being harmed. In fact, the more you deliberately practice positive ways of relating to your partner, the more spontaneous the new communications will feel to you and your partner, and the more natural they will actually be.

Caution! Don't fall into the trap of saying "Its's too mechanical," or, "If it doesn't come naturally and he has to practice, forget it," or, "If she cared enough, she would do it without reading a book or doing exercises or seeing a shrink."

Most of the following exercises can be used by either partner alone or by both together. Only a few require participation by both you and your partner.

TAKING STOCK

If you checked the boxes at the end of each trap in the last section, you have already taken the first step to change your communication pattern. This questionnaire or self-assessment inventory technique is used frequently in magazine and newspaper articles, in self-help books and in psychological research. It heightens your awareness and tends to make you think about issues you might otherwise neglect. In addition, if you come back to the list of traps at a later time and check the boxes again, you'll get some idea of your progress. The mere checking of a box takes the problem out of the *thinking* realm and puts it into the *action* realm. You have started to *do* something to change the situation, and that is what this book is about — *doing*.

If, for some reason, you haven't checked the boxes, I urge you to do it now. It won't take long and it will get you started on a sound psychological plan to make your relationship better. To simplify this task, all of the traps, with boxes to check, are listed in one place at the end of the book.

REMINDERS

Putting your relationship on a better track means learning some new habits and unlearning some old ones. Even if you want to do something new and constructive, you will probably forget to do it, unless you have practiced enough so that what you have learned has become automatic. A *reminder* is a device that can help you make these new habits part of your routine.

The Reminder can be a note in your appointment book (Tell Bill I love him, Send Nancy flowers on Saturday), a sign at home or in your place of work, a string tied around your finger or a friend calling to remind you. Again, please be careful, when your partner uses reminders, not to fall into the trap of saying, "What good is it if he has to be reminded to say nice things or to remember our anniversary? If he really felt it, he wouldn't have to be reminded." Of course, it is better if you and your partner think of these things yourselves without being reminded, but progress occurs in stages. If you use the "all or none" approach discussed in the last section (Trap #23), you will not get much satisfaction from your relationship, and you will surely have a hard time making it better. **The only thing that matters is where you want to be and how to get there.**

Many years ago a friend's wife used a *reminder* to improve his habit of leaving the bathroom sink a mess in the morning. She had tried asking nicely, and he would forget;

when she was critical, he'd feel annoyed. One day he walked into the bathroom and found a picture of Rodin's sculpture *The Kiss* taped to a corner of the mirror over the sink. A note on the picture said, "Sweetheart, thank you for cleaning up." My friend was deeply moved and felt inspired to clean up before leaving the bathroom for all the months the picture remained — and thereafter as well.

DECLARATION OF COLLABORATION

Collaborating is one of the essentials for getting along better. In order to collaborate, it is helpful to ask, "What are *we* doing wrong?" and, "What can *we* do to make it better?" Don't *ever* blame your partner for the problems or for the failure to resolve them, but rather make it a joint responsibility and effort.

A Declaration of Collaboration is a statement affirming your mutual commitment to put aside your grievances, resolve your differences and have as much fun together as possible. Make up a sentence that you will say to yourself every day or that you and your partner will recite together. One that I like to use is:

We will work together every day to
make our relationship better.

If you recite that statement aloud every morning, you will be starting the day on a positive note. Use a Reminder to strengthen this exercise. Write your statement of collaboration on a large piece of paper and post it on a closet door, a bathroom mirror or refrigerator door. Carry a wallet-size copy as well for frequent reference.

PROBLEM SOLVING APPROACH

To avoid destructive automatic reactions to your partner, it is helpful to learn a rational approach to analyzing and solving problems. The problem solving approach consists of the following three steps:

1) Ask yourself: *What do I want? What is my goal, my objective?* Is it a good relationship? A better sex life? A chance to blow off steam? Getting even?

2) Next ask: *What is the best way to get what I want?* Is it by asking nicely? Negotiating? Doing something my partner wants? Threatening? Screaming?

3) Then: Weigh the pros and the cons of doing what it takes to achieve your goal. Ask yourself: *Am I willing to do what is necessary to get what I want?* Is it worth the effort, time, money? Is it worth practicing a few exercises to be happier in my relationship? What effort am I making now? What is the risk (failure, rejection, pain)? What are the chances of achieving my goal?

Answer these questions first about your relationship in general and then about the myriad things you say and do to your partner. If you are like most of us, you will be amazed to discover that many of the things you say and do are automatic responses that make it difficult or impossible to get what you want. For example, when you are about to snarl, withdraw, reject an invitation to cuddle, refuse to visit his/her family, what are you hoping to accomplish? If possible, *before* reacting, ask yourself,"What is my objective? Are the results of my communication likely to be positive or negative? Will this statement or action bring me closer to my goal or make it harder to achieve?"

After you have said or done something to your partner, ask yourself, "What was the purpose of that communication?" Was it to hurt your partner, to get even, to make him or her feel bad, guilty, inadequate, inferior? Was it that you simply didn't want him or her to do the same hurtful things again? Was your objective to be right, **or was it to have a better relationship?**

Then ask yourself, "How close did I come to achieving my objective?" If it didn't turn out well, how could you have done it better? Think of one situation that occurred recently and, in the space below, write down how you could have handled it better.

_____

_____

_____

This one exercise, the problem solving approach, summarizes the basic message of the book: **Convert automatic irrational and negative thoughts, emotions and actions into rational, goal-directed problem solving activity.**

SELF-INSTRUCTION

How do you break a habit? How do you get yourself to do something that you are not accustomed to doing? One important way is to use Self-Instruction, a technique researched extensively by psychologist, Donald Meichenbaum. Self-Instruction simply means telling yourself to do the thing you want to do. It is different from thinking. A great deal of thinking is haphazard and is not designed to solve problems. A *thought* about doing something, or a desire to do it, or even a plan to do it, is not the same thing as *telling* yourself to do it. Thinking, "I want to make love tonight," "I wish John would ask me to make love," or even, "I should ask John to make love tonight" are all examples of self-talk, but they lack the focus of self-instruction. "Ask John to make love—now" is an example of self-instruction—telling yourself what to do.

Self-Instruction is a critical step in the chain of events leading to an activity. It often spells the difference between doing something and not doing it, between success and failure. If there is something you want to do but you feel uncomfortable about it, try giving yourself a specific instruction, for example, "Stay calm," "Eat the main course but not the rolls or dessert," "Tell Bert that he's a wonderful person."

Sounds simple, doesn't it? Self-Instruction *is* simple but it is a useful and powerful tool. If you tell yourself to do something, you are more apt to do it than if you just think about doing it.

SELF-MONITORING

Self-monitoring means observing *and* keeping a written record of habits you want to change. Observation and recording are essential skills for anyone who wants to understand events in the world. They are particularly important to scientists, to writers and to those who wish to make changes in themselves. To monitor the habits you want to change, use a pocket sized notebook. You may be familiar with this technique in connection with weight reduction or smoking cessation programs. Observing your own actions and thought patterns *and* recording them in a notebook can help bring about change. Merely observing your behavior and making a mental note is rarely enough. Why? Because thoughts are fleeting, but writing them down tends to fix them in your mind.

Here's how self-monitoring works. Suppose you have become aware of a tendency to criticize your partner (Trap #3). By writing down each instance in the notebook, you heighten your awareness of the habit and make it easier to do something about it. In the same way, if you want to get into the habit of complimenting your partner more often, make a notation in your notebook every time you *do* remember. Such an entry might read, "Sent Joan a card" or "Told Arnie what a wonderful sense of humor he has."

PRAISING YOURSELF

We hope that Joan and Arnie will respond favorably to each other's good deeds, but self-praise is more dependable. When you have complimented your partner or have done something else that is good for the relationship, say to yourself, "Well done, Joan, you did something really good!" This technique includes not only *saying* something nice to yourself but *doing* something nice for yourself (buying yourself a present, treating yourself to a massage) *after* you have taken some step to improve your relationship.

Praising yourself is not the same thing as liking yourself or being pleased about something you did. *Doing* is very different from *feeling*. This technique is a specific psychological device called self-reinforcement, and it is an important tool for strengthening habits. Think of three positive relationship habits that you would like to develop or strengthen, such as being on time for appointments, controlling your temper, or supporting your partner's leisure time activities, and write them down in the space below.

1. _____

2. _____

3. _____

From now on, whenever you do one of these things or take any action that helps your relationship, especially if it is something new, strengthen it by praising yourself.

TAPE RECORDER

In working with couples, I have found the best monitoring technique to be the tape recorder. If you don't own one, I urge you to buy one. It may be the best investment you'll ever make in your relationship. Whenever you are together, keep a small recorder handy. If your interaction is stormy, keep the machine running most of the time. If major conflicts arise only when discussing certain subjects, turn the machine on when these issues come up. If specific locations or times of day are particularly difficult, use it in those situations and at those times. If communication breakdowns occur periodically without warning, one of you may have the presence of mind to switch the machine on. Make sure that both of you agree to do this exercise. There are few things more destructive than turning the recorder on without your partner's consent in order to get the goods on him. This maneuver will only compound the damage.

A tape recorder serves two basic purposes:

1) *As a control mechanism.* It is as if someone else is listening. You are less apt to be destructive if you know that the machine is on, especially if the material is to be shared with a therapist or other person. Sometimes a patient will say, "It won't work. He'll just be on his good behavior." My answer is, "Wouldn't it be wonderful that we had found a way to prevent destructiveness? "

2) *For later study*. By listening to the tape afterwards, you become more aware of your own style and can see the traps you are involved in. The advantage of having a taped record of the conversation is that you can listen when you are in a calmer and more rational frame of mind. Useful learning is rarely accomplished in the heat of the moment, and later memories are usually distorted. Again, it is important to listen to the tape in order to learn how to improve *your* style. On the other hand, if your partner asks you to point things out about him, then by all means do so. However, the best results are achieved by focusing primarily on yourself.

There is no better way to make yourself aware of what you're doing than listening to a tape. If you have time and want to do something exceptional for yourself and your relationship, you can extend the value of the tape recorder by trying the next exercise — Analyzing The Script.

ANALYZING THE SCRIPT

If you are ambitious and willing to take the time, transcribe the tape you have made, and then go over the script line by line, identifying the traps and rewriting sentences that could have been stated more constructively. In this exercise, each partner receives a copy, and, when an outside person is consulted, three copies are used. Analyzing The Script may be the single most effective technique there is. It takes time, but it's worth it. The following is an example of a script analysis:

Harry and Fran were at a party, where someone mentioned a friend who had a gambling problem. Fran said to a group of strangers, "Harry's brother is a gambler." Harry, who is very attached to his family, shouted "What the hell is the matter with you? You are really stupid!" When they got home, Fran turned on the tape recorder.

Fran: "I am not going to tolerate abuse from you any more."

Harry: "You were really malicious about my brother. How dare you embarrass me and my family in front of strangers."

Fran: "There was nothing malicious about it. I was just stating a fact and trying to relate to those people who had a similar experience, and you got crazy."

Harry: "You owe me an apology."

Fran: *"You* are the one who owes *me* an apology. I did nothing wrong. It's your temper that's the problem."

Harry: "I may have a temper, but only when you provoke me."

Fran: "Everyone tells me what a vicious temper you have, even the people you work with."

Harry: "That's funny. Everyone tells *me* I am much calmer these days. You are the only one who complains, but that's not surprising. You complain about everything. All I hear from you is the negatives. I have never heard one word of praise for anything I have ever done."

Fran: "There hasn't been much positive, I must say. And, I've been living with this temper of yours for twenty-three years. You don't see *me* acting the way you act. Remember the Greens' party? You said my mother drinks too much. I didn't attack you—especially in public. I was brought up with manners."

Harry: "You were brought up with creeps."

IN MY OFFICE

> Fran: (to me) "Doctor, he really needs help. I have never seen a temper like his."
>
> Harry: "There is nothing wrong with me. What the hell did 12 years of therapy do for you? You still have the same rotten disposition."
>
> Fran: (to me) "Another thing, doctor, he was never a father to our children and when he did talk to them, he was always screaming."

THE ANALYSIS

Statement: Fran: "Harry's brother is a gambler."

Traps

A) Abusing a confidence by disclosing to strangers sensitive information about someone Harry is particularly close to. (#34)

B) Confusing the person with the deed. "Harry's brother has a gambling problem" or, "Harry's brother gambles a lot" would be better than "Harry's brother is a gambler." (#12)

Statement: Harry: "What the hell are you talking about? You are really stupid!"

Traps

A) Criticizing Fran. (#3)

B) Attacking Fran in public. (#3)

C) Making a negative "you" statement (#3) instead of

    1) Reporting your own feelings ("I felt hurt when you said my brother was a gambler"), or,

    2) Requesting a different approach in the future and assuming benign motives. ("Would you do something for me and not discuss my brother's problem with people who don't already know about it? I know you didn't mean any harm, but I really get upset about it.")

D) Confusing the person with the deed. (#12) ("You are stupid.") "You did a stupid thing" is slightly better. "I feel that you did a stupid thing" is slightly better still, but other communications already discussed are far more constructive. ("I was upset at what you said about my brother" is probably best of all.)

Statement: Fran: "I am not going to tolerate abuse from you any more."

Traps:

A) Implied threat. (#7)

B) Negative emotional language ("abuse"). (#15)

C) Criticizing Harry (#3) instead of

    1) Acknowledging her own contribution to the conflict. ("It was thoughtless of me." "I'm really sorry; I hope you know that I didn't mean any harm by it and I will try not to refer to it in the future.")

    2) Requesting a change in Harry's style. ("I shouldn't have mentioned his gambling, but I really have a hard time when you get so angry at me. Can we work it out so that if I do something thoughtless and hurtful in the future, you tell me that you feel hurt and ask me not to do it. I will make every effort not to do this kind of thing again.")

Statement: Harry: "You were really malicious about my brother."

Traps:

A) Criticizing Fran and not apologizing for his own intemperate remarks. (#3)

B) Another negative "you" statement. ("You were malicious...")

C) Making a malignant interpretation about Fran's motives (malice). (#47)

Statement: Fran: "There was nothing malicious about it."

Traps:

A) Contradicting Harry's perception that her remarks were destructive. (#24) It is better to acknowledge what is reasonable about his statement by saying, "I didn't mean to do that, but I can see how you feel and I'm really sorry it happened."

Statement: Fran: "You got crazy."

Traps:

A) Negative "you" statement. (#3)

B) Psychological warfare (labeling Harry "crazy"). (#18)

Statement: Harry: "You owe me an apology."

Traps:

A) Being right (#9) with a bit of moral coercion.

B) Implied blame and self-justification. (#4)

Statement: Harry: "I may have a temper, but only when you provoke me."

Traps:

A) This is a pseudo-acknowledgement; Harry seems to acknowledge his own destructiveness but actually blames Fran. (#4)

B) Not taking responsibility for his own feelings and actions. (#42) "You provoke me" is not as accurate as "I get upset" or "I allow myself to get upset."

Statement: Fran: "Everyone tells me what a vicious temper you have, even the people you work with."

Traps:

A) Quoting third parties to bolster her position. (#21)

Statement: Harry: "That's funny, everyone tells me I am much calmer these days. You are the only one who complains, but that's not surprising. You complain about everything. All I hear from you is the negatives. I have never heard one word of praise for anything I have ever done."

Traps:

A) Quoting third parties. (#21)

B) Self-justification. (#4)

C) Getting even. (#36)

D) Negative "You" statement. (#3)

E) The use of absolutes (everything, all, never, any thing, ever). (#29)

Statement: Fran: "There hasn't been much positive, I must say. And, I've been living with this temper of yours for twenty-three years. You don't see *me* acting the way you act. Remember the Greens' party? You said my mother drinks too much. I didn't attack you, especially in public. I was brought up with manners."

Traps:

A) Failure to acknowledge positives. (#23)

B) Criticizing Harry. (#3)

C) Bringing up the past. (#1)

D) Making negative comparisons. (#19)

Statement: Harry: "You were brought up with creeps."

Traps:

A) Getting even. (#36)

B) Attacking Fran's basic relationships. (#43)

C) Using negative emotional language (#15). It would be far more rational, though not particularly constructive in this instance, to say, "I don't care for certain attitudes and habits in some members of your family."

Statement: Fran: "He really needs help. I have never seen a temper like his."

Traps:

A) Psychological warfare. (#18)

B) Trying to make an ally of a third party (the therapist). (#21)

Statement: Harry: "There is nothing wrong with me. What the hell did 12 years of therapy do for you? You still have the same rotten disposition."

Traps:

A) Self-justification. (#4)

B) Getting even. (#36)

C. Attacking the person instead of dealing with the issue. (#12)

Statement: Fran: "Another thing, doctor, he was never a father to our children and, when he did talk to them, he was always screaming."

Traps:

A) Changing the subject. (Related to #22)

B) Appealing to a third party. (#21)

C) Using never and always. (#29)

D) Universalizing her own definition of father (#11) and confusing the person with the deed. (#12) Fran was suggesting that there are certain specific things that Harry didn't do that she associates with being a father.

REHEARSAL

The Rehearsal technique involves practicing what you would like to say or do in order to prepare yourself for a future event. You may already have used this technique before going to a job interview or making a presentation at work or school. If you plan to ask for a raise at your job or request a date with a person you find attractive, or give a talk, or reject pressure by a demanding friend or relative, Rehearsal will help you.

If a difficult situation is likely to come up in the near future, or if you want to discuss a topic that might lead to bad feelings, write down what you want to say to your partner *before* the confrontation. Then practice saying aloud what you have written. Rehearsal helps you prepare yourself for the real thing so that you will get your message across more clearly, and also be less tense. On the other hand, if you wait until the topic comes up or the event happens, you may be caught off guard and not have a chance to think about the best way to react. One advantage of Rehearsal is that it can be used any time you have a few minutes to practice.

Every year Paul and Liz have a fight about where to spend Christmas. He insists that they go to St. Louis to be with his family, whereas she wants to celebrate at home. Liz uses Rehearsal to prevent the usual bad scene. She writes out the following statement and then practices saying it many times to a pillow propped up in an empty chair:

Paul, I want to discuss our Christmas plans. I know it's important for you to share the holiday with your parents, and I would like to please you. But, for me, its not the same as having it at home. Your parents are really okay, but I just feel terribly uncomfortable there. Would you be willing to stay home this year? Or, maybe you could go without me and even take one of the kids. As much as I'd love being with you, it would be easier for me that way than if we all went to St. Louis.

She then pictures Paul getting furious and demanding that she go with him. At this point she rehearses in a calm voice:

I feel terrible that you're so upset. I wish there were some way we could work it out. It's hard for me to go to St. Louis every year and I would appreciate it if we could stay home this time. I'd be glad to call your parents and try to straighten it out, so they won't feel offended.

When Liz finally spoke to Paul about Christmas, she was able to say what she wanted to say calmly, rather than let the situation deteriorate into a screaming match as she had in the past. Paul was less upset than she thought he would be, largely because her presentation was so much better. He actually agreed to stay home, but even if he hadn't, Liz would have had the satisfaction of saying what she felt in an assertive, constructive way. With enough practice she would also learn not to feel guilty about disappointing him. The Rehearsal technique worked for her—as it can for you.

List two situations in your life where this technique could be useful.

1. _____

2. _____

ROLE REVERSAL

One of the big problems in relationships is the difficulty in knowing and actually feeling what it is like to be in your partner's position. Although you may have lived with the same person for 20 years, you probably don't really know what it is like to feel his or her pain, insecurities, rejection, disappointment, hopes and desires. This failure may cause you to take your partner for granted, ignore him or dismiss what is important to her. One way to get out of this subjective bind is to ask yourself the following questions: What is it like to be my partner in this relationship? What is it like for this person who is involved with me to deal with my habits, my beliefs, my actions? *Write out the answers to these questions.*

Another effective way to get this perspective is by using Role Reversal, which is taken from a form of therapy called *psychodrama*. In this technique, you act the part of your mate, taking his side, saying his lines, pleading his case, as if you were literally your partner. Since you have heard his or her routine so many times, you probably know the lines by heart, but usually the compassion and empathy are missing. Role Reversal gives you a better view of what it is like to be in your partner's shoes and it makes collaborative problem solving a lot easier. While you are playing your partner's role, he or she acts *your* role and says your lines. It is important in doing this exercise not to distort your partner's position. Don't make it sound ridiculous. Try to make the presentation as realistic as possible.

Mary (playing John's part): "Every time you don't want to do something you blame it on your period."

John (playing Mary's part): "If you cared about me, you might show a little compassion. Besides, you're a real sexist."

The role reversal exercise continues in this way for several minutes, with one or more topics being discussed. In addition to promoting greater insight, understanding and closeness, this technique can often be fun to use.

When you are alone, you can do the role reversal exercise in your head by picturing yourself saying your partner's lines. Sometimes when a patient comes to see me without a partner and describes a conflict, I ask, "What would Bill say if he were here?" When you are feeling upset, frustrated, angry or outraged, ask yourself, "How does my partner see this? How does he/she feel about it?"

There are two people in this relationship and usually two viewpoints and two sets of feelings. One of the keys to success in relationships, business as well as personal, is the ability to get into the other person's head and know what it is like to be her or him. Role reversal and related exercises will help a lot.

LAWYER EXERCISE

Sometimes I ask people to state their own positions as if they were not personally involved, but instead were their own lawyers. In this exercise, you start every statement with "My client..."

Anne: "My client would like another child."

Al: "My client understands your client's feelings in the matter but insists that he is too old to take care of another child and also assume the financial burden."

Anne: "My client is upset and angry because your client agreed to have three children when they got married and he is now backing out of that commitment."

The Lawyer Exercise keeps the discussion more on a *content* level and less on an *emotional* level.

HOW TO END A BAD SCENE

This book is partly about *preventing* trouble, but what do you do to limit the damage once a bad scene occurs? There are actually three points at which you can do something:

1) Before it starts (prevention);

2) While it is going on (termination);

3) After the flare-up (reconnection).

If possible, you want to *prevent* a bad scene from happening. You do this by being assertive instead of aggressive, by avoiding the Traps in Part Two, by developing a greater tolerance of your partner's irritating qualities, and by using all the other methods that have been discussed. One of the most important prevention techniques is *warning your partner* when you are in a bad mood or feeling particularly vulnerable and hypersensitive. At such times you might say, "I've had a lousy day and feel awful. If I snap at you, don't pay any attention." It is important to protect your partner from your destructiveness by keeping out of his way or by warning her while you still have enough control. Of course, this technique will be worthless if warnings are issued daily.

The next best thing you can do is to stop the argument or misunderstanding before more harm is done. If you recognize that you had a role in provoking or overreacting, and your ego is healthy enough, one of the best things you can do is *apologize*. An apology doesn't mean that you take full responsibility for the entire problem. It does mean that you are a big enough person to recognize that you may have made some contribution to the misunderstanding or difficulty.

Some couples use a gesture or a word such as a "TRUCE!" or "HUG!" to bridge the hostility gap. Several couples have successfully used a whistle or a party noise-maker to break the tension. Sometimes, starting to tell a joke or doing something bizarre such as rolling around on the floor will stop the unpleasant scene.

Finally, it is important to repair the damage that has been done and reconnect after the bad scene has occurred. Some years ago Hallmark aired a television commercial showing a married couple riding on a train. They had obviously had a fight and were not speaking to each other. The man took a Hallmark card out of his pocket and placed it in front of the woman, who picked it up, read it and smiled. The ice was broken. You can easily learn to do this kind of thing yourself, but **you must prevent your ego from getting in the way. It doesn't matter who started it or who's right or whose fault it is. What's important is getting the relationship back on track.** Also, don't leave it to your partner to break the stalemate; seize the initiative yourself!

While ending a bad scene or reconnecting after a bad scene are important, these measures do not solve *content* problems. Basic differences remain, and they need to be resolved, but prolonged coldness and anger is senseless and makes problem-solving impossible. Any device to interrupt irrational negative behavior is worthwhile.

RETAKE

I am sure that there have been many times when you have found yourself in the midst of a terrible scene and wondered how you ever got there, or wished that you could start over. In many cases you can do just that. The Retake technique is based on the film industry's practice of shooting a scene again when it doesn't come out right.

Make an agreement with your partner that whenever either of you wants to replay a scene, just ask for a Retake. Be sure you understand that either of you can request a retake no matter who started the trouble. For example, if you are having an argument on the phone, ask your partner if you can start over. Whoever initiated the call will dial again. DON'T pick up where you left off, but literally, start again with "Hi honey, how was your day?..." If you are having a scene at the dinner table, you might both walk out of the room and then come back to the table and start over. In some instances, going outside of the house or apartment and coming through the front door again provides an opportunity for a fresh start.

THE HUGGING EXERCISE

Make an agreement that you will hug each other for fifteen seconds twice a day, once in the morning and once in the evening. *This exercise has nothing to do with how you feel about each other,* but it is a way of putting aside indifference and hostility and beginning a more positive life together. You may think that you loathe your partner, but for some reason you have chosen to hang in there. Why not make it as tolerable as possible? Besides, since **behavior change precedes feeling change**, you might even be able to improve the way you feel about each other.

If you have an interest in getting along better, it is useful to program positive experiences into your life together. This recommendation does not mean that you should always pretend everything is fine while avoiding basic problems. It does mean that you can start changing your relationship immediately by practicing less destructive ways of *acting* toward each other, no matter how you feel initially. Even if you have to swallow hard, hold your nose and make a face, try the Hugging Exercise.

COMMUNICATING IN WRITING

Your relationship may be so negative that it is impossible to talk at all without causing more trouble. In that case try Communicating in Writing for short periods of time. In this exercise, both of you carry a pad of paper and a pen at all times. The advantage of this technique is that it is harder to be destructive when writing than speaking, because the emotional intensity is not the same. If you and your partner are able to cooperate on this issue, you can decide to speak only when you have something positive or neutral to say, and write whenever you have something negative to convey.

Lester and Natalie had explosive arguments when discussing several topics, such as their son's difficulties at school (they would blame each other), buying a new house (she wanted to, he didn't), having another child, his mother's meddling in their lives, and his trips to the racetrack. They couldn't make any progress because they never got past the first sentence without an outburst. After agreeing to communicate in writing, they exchanged the following notes:

Natalie: "I would like us to see a child psychiatrist about Billy's school problem."

Lester: "He doesn't need a psychiatrist. You're always looking for doctors. If you didn't push him so much, he'd be fine and outgrow it. I was the same way at his age."

Natalie: "I would really appreciate your going once with me. I just want to get a professional opinion. We don't even have to take the advice if you don't want to."

Lester: "Maybe once, but that's it."

Natalie: "Thanks."

WHISPERING

A related exercise that defuses hostility is Whispering, especially when you are talking about charged issues. If, for example, you fight whenever you discuss the choice between buying a washer-dryer and a stereo, or where to spend the next vacation, don't discuss the topic unless you whisper.

Make a list of all the explosive issues you can think of, and use the Whispering technique to help you deal with them.

Explosive Issues

1. _____

2. _____

3. _____

4. _____

5. _____

Whispering is one of the exercises you can use yourself if your partner is unwilling to try it. You will find that it is more difficult for your partner to shout if you are whispering. This way of communicating not only reduces animosity, but it may actually be quite sexy. Again, whispering is not a substitute for resolving basic problems but remember, *style precedes content*. That is to say, you'll make a lot more progress resolving issues (content) if the style of communicating is constructive.

HASSLE-FREE ACTIVITY

In the same way that certain *issues* seem to produce tension, you may have noticed that particular *activities* and *locations* seem to cause trouble. Sometimes, despite good intentions, you and your partner may become irritable or have a fight for no apparent reason. In these cases you may be able to improve the situation by changing some of the things you do together and by changing where you do others.

To apply the Hassle-Free Activity technique to your relationship, make a list of all the places you go, people with whom you spend time, and activities you engage in together. Note which of these activities are connected with tension and conflict and which are associated with closeness and pleasantness. Arrange to spend as much time in the hassle-free activities and as little time in the conflict situations as possible. If socializing with others causes no tension, then do it more. If playing tennis, or going to the movies, or going out to dinner, or staying home to watch television are not connected with bad feelings or open conflict, then do those activities more. If you find that you are fighting a lot at the dinner table, eat out more often if you can afford it, or eat in front of the television set. If a fight starts as soon as one of you walks in the door, then greet each other outside, or meet somewhere after work and then go home together. If you notice that you are fighting a lot in the bedroom, see if you can use the bedroom just for sleeping, but watch television and even make love in another room.

MAKING IT AS A COUPLE

Low Hassle Activities and Locations	High Hassle Activities and Locations
1._____	1._____
2._____	2._____
3._____	3._____
4._____	4._____
5._____	5._____
6._____	6._____

LISTING PARTNER'S POSITIVES

A great deal of difficulty in relationships is caused by:

1) the difference between what you expect from your partner and what you get from your partner;

2) focusing on what you are missing rather than what you are getting.

To help you develop a better perspective on your relationship, make a list of all your partner's positive qualities. Doing this exercise doesn't mean that you should overlook important negatives. The goal is to be sure that you appreciate the positive qualities and give credit where it is due.

A man who came to me for therapy had been highly critical of his wife and, at times, verbally abusive as well. She became emotionally detached and unwilling to have sex with him. When asked to list her positive qualities, he was stumped; he couldn't think of a single desirable attribute. After much deliberation and some prodding, he came up with a list of fourteen including:

- intelligent
- honest
- contributes substantially to the family income
- a good mother
- affectionate
- sexy

To be sure, she had her limitations. She was critical of him and rarely praised his worthy deeds. Repeated reference to the list helped him develop a different view of her, and he began treating her better. She in turn responded.

Use this page to start your list:

Partner A's List of B's Positive Qualities	Partner B's List of A's Positive Qualities
1._____	1._____
2._____	2._____
3._____	3._____
4._____	4._____
5._____	5._____

Now ask yourself the following questions:

I. Do you appreciate these positive qualities you've listed?

PARTNER A   YES ☐ NO ☐ NOT ENOUGH ☐
PARTNER B   YES ☐ NO ☐ NOT ENOUGH ☐

II. Do you *tell* your partner that you appreciate these qualities?

PARTNER A   YES ☐ NO ☐ NOT ENOUGH ☐
PARTNER B   YES ☐ NO ☐ NOT ENOUGH ☐

Remember, if you want to deal effectively with problems, no matter what they may be, it's a good idea to start with the positives.

In troubled relationships, partners are more apt to take each other's positive qualities for granted. If you want your relationship to improve, make the list and then tell your partner that you appreciate these qualities. Even if you feel hurt, bitter and resentful, your partner still possesses these positive attributes. Acknowledge them.

THE LISTENING EXERCISE

Among the most important skills for developing a good social life and enjoying a positive relationship with your partner are listening and responding.

Many years ago there was a parlor game in which a player was not permitted to speak until he/she repeated verbatim what the previous speaker had said. It was good training in listening. In The Listening Exercise, ask your partner at least one question per day that indicates some interest in what he/she is doing. This exercise will be particularly helpful if one or both of you feel that the other doesn't listen. After your partner responds to the question, repeat what she said to show that you were listening. It would go something like this this:

Frank:	"How did things go at work today?"
Edith:	"It was very hectic. For one thing Tina got a promotion."
Frank:	"Tina got a promotion? How did she react to the news?"

You can see that the listening exercise has three steps:

1) Showing an interest by asking a question (initiation);

2) After partner responds, repeat what she said (restatement);

3) Ask a follow-up question in order to show that your interest is being maintained (continuation).

If your *partner* is the one who isn't a good listener, don't assume he or she doesn't care. While it is true that sometimes people don't ask how your day went because they don't care, often it is simply a matter of a good habit that was never cultivated. *Feeling* and *behavior* are separate realms. You can care very deeply about someone and not respond to what he is saying.

If you are not always attentive to what your partner says, practice The Listening Exercise as a way of demonstrating your interest. If your partner sometimes seems to ignore you, make the benign assumption about why it happens, and work together to improve the situation by using The Listening Exercise.

NEGOTIATING TIME

To further reduce spontaneous discussion of highly charged topics and minimize the airing of resentment throughout the week, set aside a prescribed period of time for discussion and negotiation. That way, whenever you are upset or angry about something or want to discuss a touchy issue, you will wait until the agreed-upon time. It can be fifteen minutes three times a week or half an hour once a week, whatever seems sufficient. Don't make it too long at first, or the session is apt to degenerate, and be sure you stop when the time is up. Open-ended discussions often deteriorate. A good time to do this exercise is when you are not in a hurry and not likely to be distracted by children or phone calls.

In addition to Negotiating Time, when major issues are approached in a problem-solving atmosphere, separate *gripe time* is helpful to some couples. During gripe time, partners complain to each other about everything that bothers them. In both of these exercises, as soon as the allotted time is up, stop the discussion and adjourn the meeting until the next scheduled session. Again, the point is to make as much of the week conflict-free as possible and to discourage spontaneous destructiveness. If you find it difficult to do this exercise in a constructive way, try it with the tape recorder running. Some couples have their negotiating sessions only in the presence of a therapist or other impartial person.

182

CONTRACTS

In every relationship, there are unspoken understandings and agreements: "We both work, and share expenses and the domestic chores;" or, "A works full time, B works part time and B does more of the cooking and household chores, but A does the dishes, mows the lawn and shovels snow in the winter;" or, "I see your family and you visit mine." These implied contracts break down over time for a variety of reasons. One of you begins to do less of what you were doing before, and the other begins to do certain things differently. One partner may gain a great deal of weight, the other may start smoking, one may take a job that involves a lot of traveling, the person who arrives home first at the end of the day may no longer come to the door to greet the other, one may begin trumpet lessons to the discomfort of the other, one partner's interest in sex may wane.

A technique I have used with great success is The Written Contract. Most of your misunderstandings and incompatibilities can be approached by negotiation, compromise and written contracts. A written document can help prevent the misinterpretations and differing recollections that often occur with verbal agreements.

Bill complains a lot about visiting Lucy's family, and Lucy resents Bill's pressuring her to go to hockey games. Each feels imposed upon by the other, but both would rather spend time together than go off on their own. Their contract reads, "Bill agrees to visit Lucy's family once a month without complaining, and Lucy agrees to attend any sporting event of Bill's choosing once a month." Both sign the contract.

If this *simple* contract doesn't work, you can use a *contingency* contract, in which there is a reward for compliance and a penalty for violations. Bill, who frequently comes home late from work, agrees to come home by 7:00 p.m. three nights a week, and Lucy agrees to give him a back rub on those nights. If he is not home by 7:00 p.m., he agrees to call her parents that night and have a ten minute conversation with them (or prepare dinner, clean up, watch her favorite television show, etc.). Again, the agreement is put in writing. Contracts work best when both partners are willing to make a good faith effort. A note of caution: be careful not to change the contract without first discussing it with your partner, and never withhold sex when applying a penalty.

DESENSITIZATION

People react in different ways and in different degrees to things their partners say and do. If your partner accidently breaks a dish, you might say, "Forget it, it's nothing," or you might shower him/her with abuse. The intensity of your reaction depends on how irritable your nervous system is and how tolerant you are of differences between the way things are and the way you want or expect them to be.

There are hundreds of differences between you and your partner—biological, psychological and social. The ability to live comfortably with your partner's political beliefs, friendships, personal habits, sexual needs, food preferences and recreational interests is a critical ingredient in successful relationships. Some of us have a very low degree of tolerance, some are highly tolerant, and some actually welcome and enjoy difference as a way of sharing, growing and learning. We learn much more from difference and diversity than from sameness.

One of the best techniques for reducing your irritability and increasing your tolerance is called Desensitization.

Everybody overreacts to something. You and your partner have triggers that set you off, things that you are overly sensitive about, events that lead to emotional upset or destructive retaliation. You and your partner are probably the world's authorities on what sets each other off. It could be that she bites her nails, or he leaves his socks on the floor, or he frequently takes phone calls from his brother during dinner, or she comes home late from seeing her friends, or he burns the food when he cooks, or he turns over and falls asleep immediately after intercourse, or she is friendly with former boyfriends, or he falls asleep in front of the television set, or he watches football all day on Sunday, or, when they go out, his clothes don't match, or her brassiers are hanging in the shower, or he leaves shaving cream all over the sink, or she leaves the lights on and wastes electricity or doesn't close the toothpaste, etc., etc.

If you are going to improve your relationship, you need to do two things:

1) Tolerate your partner's habits and faults better than you do now;

2) Learn how to get your partner to change.

If you don't do these two things, nothing will happen. The same patterns will continue, the same ineffective remedies will be tried, and the same apathy, indifference, boredom, hostility, suffering and self-deception will result.

This chapter is about the first issue, increasing your tolerance, and the next section deals with ways of getting your partner to change. **Both of these steps are essential— one is not enough.** This entire book has one basic theme:

changing the sensitivity and reactions of one partner *and* changing the behavior of the other partner.

You don't need to accept everything your partner does in order to be happy, but you do have to learn to accept a lot—especially if no real harm is being done. Not only must you learn to accept your partner's behavior, but you must also learn not to upset yourself about it. The powerful psychological technique called Desensitization is the key to this process. Before reading further, think about this basic point:

While it is always better when both of you can work together on these projects, you can also work successfully on them *entirely on your own*—without any cooperation at all from your partner.

This principle frees you from the fatal trap of putting the responsibility on your partner for turning things around.

The word desensitization means *decreasing* your sensitivity to outside events, or even to your own thoughts. The technique has been used by allergists for most of this century to cure people of abnormal sensitivities to food, pollen, dust, animal dander and many other substances. Similarly, psychologists since the 1920's have been desensitizing people to *psychological* irritants. Thousands of people have been successfully treated for irrational fears (heights, elevators, harmless snakes, etc.) with this technique.

The first step is to make a list of all the things you can think of in the relationship that set you off or turn you off. I should really say, "The things *you allow* to set you off," because **events don't control us—we** *allow* **them to control us.** Write out a list of all the things you can think of that lead you to destructive overreaction. If you have trouble doing this, you may get some ideas from the examples on the previous page.

Again, it is better, although not necessary, to do this exercise as a team since two of you will probably come up with more items than one of you alone. However you do it, do it *now* before going on. It will take only a few minutes, and the list doesn't have to be complete. You can always add items later.

What I overreact to (Partner A)

1. _____

2. _____

3. _____

4. _____

5. _____

What I overreact to   (Partner B)

1. _____

2. _____

3. _____

4. _____

5. _____

If you now look at the list, you will see that most of these issues are either minor (they do not inherently cause great inconvenience) or symbolic (they don't cause any harm or inconvenience at all—it's just that you don't like them). If Dave leaves the toilet seat up in the middle of the night and Wendy falls in, that is somewhat unpleasant, but if she gets upset simply because she *might* have fallen in, that is a destructive overreaction. Minor and symbolic issues can often be resolved by using desensitization, whereas issues of greater importance usually have to be negotiated.

Desensitization does *not* mean that you suppress your feelings, grit your teeth and go along with things you hate. It *does* mean learning to *feel* less upset about many irritants. The value of Desensitization is that it enables you to pay less attention to minor issues and reduces your strong negative emotional feelings about major ones so that you can handle them more rationally. In the same way that an allergist desensitizes you to ragweed by injecting you repeatedly with small and then larger doses of the pollen, you deliberately expose yourself to your partner's irritating habit. For example, as an exercise, you might ask your partner to say disparaging things about your mother, or have him deliberately leave his socks and underwear on the floor near the bed. If you are not getting along well enough to collaborate on this exercise, there are two ways of *desensitizing yourself.*

1) Practice doing the very things that irritate you when your partner does them. For example, if you hate uncapped toothpaste, deliberately leave it uncapped yourself. Or, if it bugs you when your partner makes you late for a social engagement, make yourself late. It's unlikely that anything terrible will happen, unless you miss the plane for your two week European vacation. In cases where this method of desensitization is not practical, try the following technique.

2) Use *mental pictures,* or *imagery.* Imagery simply refers to the mind's ability to form pictures. Dreams are mental pictures that occur during sleep, and fantasies or daydreams are mental pictures that occur when you are awake. *Imagery therapy* is the deliberate use of mental pictures to bring about desired changes in your attitudes, feelings and behavior.

Here is an example of *imagery desensitization:*

> Milton had a terrible temper and frequently screamed at
> Amy. Although there was no danger of physical vio-
> lence, she trembled in fear of his outbursts. She was
> able to rid herself of the fear by doing the following
> exercises for one minute several times a day over a two
> week period. With her eyes closed, she pictured Milton
> screaming at her. While "seeing" Milton screaming,
> she pictured herself remaining absolutely calm. In the
> second exercise, she again pictured Milton screaming at
> her, but then imagined toning down his volume, so that
> after a few seconds she "heard" him speaking in a nor-
> mal tone, then talking softly, then whispering, and fi-
> nally moving his lips with no sound coming out. An-
> other helpful exercise is to picture an abusive partner
> with marbles in his/her mouth.

To use *imagery desensitization,* follow these four basic
steps:

1) Sit in a comfortable position, close your eyes, take a
   few slow, deep breaths, and imagine any scene that
   you find relaxing (e.g., walking in the woods, lying
   on a beach, lounging in a hammock).

2) Now picture your partner doing the thing that irri-
   tates, upsets or frightens you.

3) Picture yourself remaining calm while he or she is doing it.

4) Picture your partner in a less threatening way (inaudible, marbles in mouth, two feet tall, sitting on the toilet, or standing 100 or 200 feet away from you).

People who have lived together for several years often become desensitized to their partner's annoying habits simply through repeated exposure, but these imagery exercises allow you to direct the process yourself and get results more quickly. Some people are better at imagery than others, and there are many exercises to use. If you would like to pursue this important technique further, you might look at books listed in the references that are devoted to this topic.

In addition to decreasing your sensitivity to your partner's undesired habit, you also want to *increase* your sensitivity to his or her desirable qualities and actions. When you put it all together, you have something like this: Howard leaves dirty dishes in the sink and Ellie gets upset about it. Ellie becomes less upset by desensitizing herself to Howard's habit (1: deliberately allows dishes to pile up herself and 2: pictures herself remaining calm when Howard leaves the sink full of dishes). She also gets Howard to clean up more often by asking him pleasantly *and* by praising him when he makes an effort. In addition, she makes a point of supporting his other positive qualities.

CHANGING YOUR PARTNER'S NEGATIVE BEHAVIOR

Introduction

I have repeatedly urged you to look at your own traps rather than your partner's, but there are times when your partner's actions are clearly destructive or just unpleasant. The best way to react depends on how important the issue is, how often the behavior occurs, how unpleasant it is, and whether it does any real harm. Obviously, the more damaging your partner's habit and the more frequently it occurs, the more important it is for you to try to change it. Just be sure that when you are looking at your partner's actions, you don't confuse what you dislike with what is wrong or irrational.

When attempting to influence your partner's actions, there are several types of changes that you can try to bring about. You may want to get your partner to:

1) do something *new* (something she or he hasn't done before such as going dancing or bowling);

2) do *more* of something you like, such as complimenting you;

3) do *less* of what you dislike, such as drinking or complaining;

4) *stop* doing what you dislike, such as hitting the children or smoking cigarettes.

It is easy to react to your partner without thinking—to get upset, outraged, depressed, disgusted, vengeful, turned off. But it is much more effective to figure out what you want, what you don't want, and how to go about changing your partner's behavior.

There are four questions you should ask yourself before reacting to negative things your partner says or does:

1) Does it cause *real* harm?

2) Is it his/her basic nature to act this way, or do these negative things happen only occasionally? To be sure, there may be one-time occurrences that are catastrophic, but it is important to know the difference between *situational* and *characterological*. Is it his/her continuing pattern (*characterological*) to be nasty, to withdraw when you want to talk, to be seductive with others? Or, is this behavior *out of character*? Situational and characterological problems are totally different and should not be treated the same way.

3) What is my objective? To get along better? To see that it doesn't happen again? To get even? To blow off steam?

4) What's the big picture? What are the pluses and minuses in the relationship as a whole? How significant is this incident in the total relationship?

Remember that a great deal of behavior is learned and can be unlearned. You and your partner learn from each other and can teach each other how to change old habits and acquire new ones. Always keep in mind the *two-person* view of problems. Your partner does something, and you react. The problem has two parts—the action and the reaction. For example, your partner may say something insulting, and you get angry. Or, you tell your partner you're going to have dinner with a friend and he or she has a jealous fit. Or, your partner has a habit of being late for appointments and you get upset. It is often not enough to expect, hope or even ask your partner to change. You need to know how to bring about this change.

Using the exercises already discussed, you can reduce the destructive impact of your partner's undesirable behavior by:

1) changing your attitude about it;

2) making sure you don't react strongly to symbolic issues;

3) desensitizing yourself to irrational behavior that does no real harm;

4) avoiding spiteful retaliation.

The major goal is to limit damage. It takes two of you to have a misunderstanding or a fight. If you can remain in control and not take the irrational negatives personally, you are in a powerful position to reduce the hurt to yourself and to the relationship.

There is a saying that people who can control themselves can control the world. Although you can tell yourself that your partner should change, *it is up to you* to create a climate in which your partner is more likely to do what you want.

How to do it:

There are 3 basic ways of getting your partner to stop destructive or undesirable behavior:

1) An assertive request for change

2) Ignoring the behavior

3) Encouraging, agreeing with, or imitating the behavior (Paradoxical Communication)

1) ASSERTIVENESS

One of the most popular ideas in modern psychology is the concept of assertiveness. Therapists teach it to individual patients, to groups, or to classes. Assertiveness is simply the ability to say what's on your mind and to act in your own interest, while respecting the rights and feelings of others. It includes initiating conversations and relationships, asking for what you want, stating your feelings, graciously declining unwelcome invitations or requests, and resisting exploitation.   Partners who have a high level of assertiveness usually provide and receive much more gratification and have less pain than those without this quality.

Psychologists distinguish between *assertiveness*, *unassertiveness* and *aggressiveness*.   Unassertiveness means that you don't express desires and feelings, either because you don't know how or because you are too uncomfortable doing so. People are said to be acting aggressively when they exploit others or trample on their feelings. Many errors in Part Two of the book illustrate different ways of being aggressive in relationships. People who are unassertive are more likeable than those who act aggressively, but they are usually as unhappy, or more so. Most of us are not all one way or the other. We act more assertively in some situations than in others.

Another side of assertiveness is self-protection. Many "me first" people feel that to be true to themselves, they shouldn't do what they don't want to do. When thinking about assertiveness, consider these important points:

1) Assertiveness does not mean saying "no" compulsively, as a matter of principle. In fact, it doesn't mean saying "no" at all. Saying "no" in intimate relationships is actually destructive, as discussed in Part Two. Assertiveness does mean the *capacity* to resist exploitation, psychological coercion and manipulation in a non-aggressive way, without experiencing anxiety or guilt. People who find it necessary or desirable to stick up for their rights at every opportunity usually don't make very good partners.

2) Reciprocity is a basic issue. There is nothing wrong with making sacrifices and concessions to please your partner, provided that there is mutuality and reciprocity—that is, where both of you act similarly toward each other.

Asking your partner to change is often a delicate matter, especially if she/he is overly sensitive to criticism. That is why it is so important to be supportive and make it easy for your partner to do what you are asking. These are some of the steps that will help accomplish the objective:

1) Start with the positives. (I see how you could feel that way, I see what you mean, I agree with this par-

ticular point, there are many wonderful things that you do and I appreciate them, I really love you a lot...);

2) Assume benign motives. (I know you don't mean any harm by it, I know it wasn't intentional...);

3) Acknowledge your own contribution to the two party communication process. (I know I can be overbearing at times, I may be overreacting, I tend to be overly sensitive about these things, perhaps I should have mentioned it sooner...);

4) Request a change in the future rather than focusing on what you don't like in the present. (Would you do this for me, I would appreciate it if..., It would mean a lot to me if...Would you be willing to try it the other way for a while?).

It obviously isn't necessary to incorporate all of these steps every time you want your partner to make some changes, but it is important to create a climate in which your partner feels supported and not threatened.

Other assertive statements include requests for clarification, for definitions of negative labels, for specific examples, or for partner's criteria for the desired behavior. When your partner says something destructive, such as "You are undependable," instead of getting upset, ask him/her one or more of the following questions:

1) "Could you tell me what you mean by 'undependable'?" (Definition/Clarification)

2) "Could you give me examples?"

3) "What would make you feel that I was dependable?" (Criteria for desired behavior)

Assertiveness is a skill like any other, and to master it requires practice. I know it's not easy for everyone to become more assertive, and if you would like additional practice in developing this important skill, I have listed some excellent references at the end of the book.

2) IGNORING

Many undesirable habits are strengthened by the attention they get from other people. In the typical *game* interaction, your partner does something you don't like and you get angry, upset or depressed, or else you retaliate. It may seem that whatever you try doesn't work.

If your partner says or does something that you honestly feel is negative, damaging or destructive, try *ignoring* it. If your partner calls you an idiot, you can act as if you didn't hear what he said and pay no attention. At first this may be difficult to do, and you may even notice that the negative behavior temporarily increases, because your partner is used to getting a reaction from you and may unconsciously try to get you to respond in the expected way. Before using this technique, you will find it helpful to practice the earlier exercises of *imagery rehearsal* and *imagery desensitization*. Using these techniques will help you control your emotions so you can use *ignoring* more effectively.

Some of the ways of *ignoring* are: being silent; excusing yourself and going to another room; going out for a walk; changing the topic; or involving yourself in some other activity such as watching television. It is essential when ignoring your partner's behavior or removing yourself from his/her presence to do it without showing any anger or resentment. If your partner wants to know where you are going, you can simply say that you want to lie down, get some fresh air, go to the bathroom or check on the baby. *It is absolutely necessary that you not be rude or critical or defensive;* all you want to do is to interrupt the pattern of negativity. In addition the *ignoring technique* will be of no value whatsoever unless you make sure to support and praise your partner when you notice improvement in the behavior you want him/her to change or when he/she is acting positively in other areas.

Note that this approach is very different from the *assertive* option. ("I know that you are angry, and I would like to listen to what you have to say, but I would appreciate it if you would talk to me a kinder way.")

Behavior fluctuates. Sometimes it's positive and sometimes it's negative. **If you ignore negative behavior and respond positively to desirable behavior, you will usually get more of the latter and less of the former.** Failure to respond to positive behavior will create the impression that you are not simply ignoring the negative *behavior* but ignoring your partner. This is why it is so important to use the technique correctly.

3) ENCOURAGING, AGREEING WITH, OR IMITATING THE BEHAVIOR
(Paradoxical Communication)

Before discussing the most fascinating and often dramatically effective technique of Paradoxical Communication, we need to talk about a type of interaction and communication pattern called a *game*. When communications specialists use the term *game*, they are not talking about recreational activities, but about a particular type of behavior pattern involving two or more people. Eric Berne, who founded the school of therapy called Transactional Analysis, wrote several books, including *Games People Play*. He distinguished the *intimacy* level from the *game* level. When people operate on the intimacy level, they are direct, honest, open, disclosing, sharing, and not competitive, hostile, defensive, judgmental or guilt-inducing. In a game, behavior is automatic, repetitive, stereotyped, predictable, irrational, unrelated to solving the problem at hand, and usually destructive. The real message is never stated clearly.

These game patterns often last a lifetime. One partner may be the persecutor and the other the victim; one may be in the helpless role and the other the protector; one may get into trouble frequently and the other repeatedly bails him out; one clings, the other withdraws.

Beth makes minor errors, Jack screams, and then Beth cries. Harvey goes out with other women, Karen finds out about it, gets very upset and threatens to leave him, whereupon he buys her an expensive present and she forgives him—until the next time. George wants to make love to Sharon, but she puts him off with a variety of excuses. Walter says repeatedly that he wants Alice to be successful in her Wall Street career, but he actually feels threatened by her success and unconsciously does everything to thwart it. When she has a business meeting at night and he is supposed to babysit, he makes other plans.

**It takes two people to create a game
but it takes only one person to stop it.**

One of the most successful ways of changing your partner's behavior, breaking up a destructive game pattern (accusing/denying, threatening/appeasing, being sick/caretaking) and even promoting greater closeness is to actually encourage the behavior you want to eliminate. This technique is called Paradoxical Communication.

A paradoxical response is a reaction that is totally different from the reactions that you and your partner expect from each other. Instead of asking that the game not be played (assertive) or simply not playing the game (ignoring), you use a communication that *changes* the game. Probably the most common paradoxical response is to agree with your partner's irrational or destructive communication.

A: "You are dumb."
B: "I know, and I'm very worried about it."

Can you see how much better it is for Partner B to look at A's comment clinically instead of getting upset and saying, "Look's who's talking," or, "Don't talk to me that way, I don't like it"? The paradoxical approach is often completely disarming. It stops the game and frequently provides comic relief. But this too must be done without the anger or hostility or sarcasm that often accompanies attempts at humor. With a paradoxical communication, you take control of an irrational situation by being equally irrational or even more irrational yourself. If your partner blames you, you can accept full responsibility not only for what you are accused of, but for other things as well. Or, if your partner repeatedly badgers you with requests for reassurance, tell him how inadequate he is.

A: "Do you think I'm homely?"
B: "I can't bear to look."

In addition to agreeing with something that is irrational, you can imitate the destructive behavior yourself. For example, Matt had a habit of coming home later than he said he would. Marge had asked him to tell her so she could make plans and not worry. She tried many ways, reasonable as well as irrational. Nothing had worked. One night when he said he'd be home for dinner at 6:00 and still hadn't arrived or called by 8:00, Marge went out. Matt arrived home at 8:20 expecting dinner and found no wife and no dinner. At first he was put out, then concerned, and by midnight panic stricken. He called every relative and friend he could think of, but no one had a clue as to Marge's whereabouts. By 12:30 the police had been notified and all of the local hospital emergency rooms telephoned. When Marge finally returned after an enjoyable dinner and a late movie, Matt was livid. She greeted him pleasantly, and promptly went to bed. He never again stayed out late without calling.

Another paradoxical technique is to encourage your partner to do more of what he is doing (e.g., urge him to stay out later). Or, you can do something that is completely bizarre to disrupt the game pattern, such as falling down on the floor and pretending to faint, or starting to mumble to yourself. If your normal style is to suffer silently, breaking a dish or two may stop the game. Paradoxical Communication is so effective that I have expanded the discussion of this important subject into a book called *Making Things Better by Making Them Worse*, from which the following examples are taken.

Pete had been complaining to Sally about his job, which was boring and paid him less than he thought he deserved. He talked constantly about getting out but did nothing about it. Sally reminded him periodically of his vow to look for a new position, but he procrastinated and continued to complain. One September day in my office he said, "Maybe in January I'll start looking." Instead of responding with her usual angry impatience, she said, "Don't rush it. I think it would be much better to wait until June or even September of next year. It's not a good idea to do anything in haste." From that point on, the change in her attitude from nagging to encouraging him to procrastinate even longer resulted in his starting a freelance business in addition to his job. A marked decrease in his complaining followed this initiative.

Lisa fears for her life every time she's a passenger in the family car. Jeff drives as if the streets of midtown Manhattan are the Indianapolis racetrack. Sudden application of the brakes immediately followed by rapid acceleration make her a prime candidate for whiplash. If another car or pedestrian blocks his way, Jeff deafens her with obscenities. Lisa suffers in silence until it becomes unbearable and then she screams at him. The problem was brought under control rather quickly by the following strategy:

Before he had a chance to curse a driver or pedestrian who was in the way, she would start cursing that person. Thus, when they were stuck behind a timid, inexperienced driver who was blocking them because he couldn't maneuver between a parked car on one side and a double-parked car on the other, she screamed, "You stupid idiot! Why the hell don't you learn how to drive?" She then started to open the door and in a determined tone said to her husband, "Let's go over there and beat him up." Jeff looked at her for a moment, then burst into laughter. He had finally gotten the point, and from then on was better able to control his temper while driving.

A male patient of mine tried a novel paradoxical approach.

Wife:	"You are just like your mother."
Husband:	(Goes to dresser drawer and starts putting on one his wife's brassieres.)

PASSION EXERCISES

We've talked about ways of reducing hostility, anger and distance, and promoting better communication. The focus has been on the *thinking* and *action* parts of your personality. When you reduce negative interactions and treat each other in a more respectful and caring way, existing positive feelings will get stronger, and positive feelings that have been dormant will become unblocked. But what about those relationships that have never had much passion, where there have never been intense feelings of enthusiasm, warmth, excitement, lust and expectancy? Many people in passionless relationships express intense feelings for such pursuits as sports, music or politics. Some feel and express passion for animals but not people; others for children but not adults; still others for friends and relatives but not for their mates.

An important question raised by some therapists is whether passion can be taught. My answer is that it can be, to some extent. If you are one of those who have not experienced much joy and passion, a few suggestions may be helpful. In trying to learn to be more passionate, it is important to know what passion is, particularly to know it when you see it. One of the most valuable ways of learning anything is to observe others. Think about people you know who are passionate. Observe what these people are doing, as if you are an actor learning from a master. Try to imitate them. It may be awkward at first, but it's a good way to learn.

Many years ago I dated a woman who bubbled constantly. She exuded warmth and compassion, hugging, kissing and loving almost every living thing she met. To this day, when I think of passion, I think of her.

The entire range of your positive emotions, fantasies and sensory experiences come into play in the process of toning up your passion. Consider this sensory exercise: Some people who want a snack will take a piece of fruit, perhaps an apple, and quickly devour it. Others, who are more sensuous, enjoy the magnificent color, study the extraordinary shape, take in the aroma and, only then, savor the taste of this luscious fruit. For some people a sexual experience seems mechanical and lasts five minutes; others spend hours touching, hugging, kissing, tickling, giggling, tasting, smelling. At one extreme we have the logical, cerebral person and the action-oriented "doers"; at the other end of the spectrum we have the emotional, intensely feeling, passionate dreamers. This book is largely about people who react before they think, but you may be one of those people who thinks too much before he/she reacts.

If you are less feeling or less expressive than you would like to be, start by making a list of all of the emotional words that you can think of. When you are engaged in any physical activity, focus on the body sensations, such as the feeling of wind blowing against your cheeks or the rain beating on your face, or the tingling sensations in a hot tub. Spend five minutes doing the apple exercise mentioned above, focusing closely on the color, shape, aroma and taste. Then tell yourself how beautiful, delicious, and succulent this piece of fruit is. Practice using intense and vivid words like "tingling" and "exciting". If you like to dance, try doing it with greater abandon. If not, take a few lessons or listen to music and try to imitate the body movements of people who dance. If you are intellectual, practice reading plays aloud, especially those with great dramatic intensity. If you are not the literary type, practice reading anything—grisly or amorous news stories, or even comic books aloud to your partner, to the wall or to an empty chair. Get a book on the art and techniques of body massage and, working with your partner, give each other a massage once a week. Practice touching each other, with your eyes closed and then open.

Try the following *emotion expression exercise:* you and your partner say to each other in a soft voice, "I hate you" and gradually repeat it with increasing volume until you're screaming. Then say in a loud voice, "I love you" and repeat this sentence, gradually lowering your voice until you are talking in a whisper. If you have difficulty communicating fantasies to your partner, first practice saying them aloud to yourself, then write them down. After lots of practice, write them to your partner. Finally, speak them to your partner. We all have a fear of rejection and ridicule, and it requires a willingness to take risks in order to unblock and learn how to become more expressive. If you're not in touch with the fantasies you have, or else find it too difficult to express them, make one up as if you were writing a movie script or playing a character in a story. Positive passion often spells the difference between an acceptable relationship and a rich relationship.

NEGATIVE PASSION

Aggression is part of our biological makeup. It is built into the brain. Rage is seen in animals, infants and in the rest of us if we are sufficiently provoked or have certain neurological illnesses. While it is certainly not a good idea to keep negative feelings bottled up, expressing anger directly can also be damaging. What is most important is *how* and *when* to express negative feelings. It is almost always better to express these feelings assertively rather than aggressively, especially in intimate relationships. But sometimes we are too blocked and have trouble showing our emotions. We may think things to death and have trouble expressing what we feel as easily as we would like to. If this is the case, aggression expression exercises, which are planned, anger expression sessions can be very useful. Remember, they are only exercises. Spontaneous outbursts of anger are usually destructive in intimate relationships, especially when the relationships are not going well.

To do this exercise, set aside one minute a day for screaming at each other. Make sure that you put each other down, insult each other, and dredge up the entire grievance list from the past 20 years—be as destructive as possible. Deliberately violate all of the rules in this book. At the end of the minute, you may both be laughing, but, in any event, hug each other. This exercise may be done with both of you shouting at the same time, or, if one is more timid than the other, take turns, with each of you having one minute of uninterrupted tirade. The person receiving the abuse must remain absolutely silent until it is his or her turn. The reasons this exercise is so helpful are:

1) You get feelings out rather than keeping them bottled up.

2) By expressing the feelings in a controlled setting you are taking the first step toward reducing their spontaneous occurrence.

3) Through repeated exposure to your partner's anger in this planned exercise, you become desensitized to his or her negative style and content. You become less apt to take destructive communications personally.

4) By exaggerating the anger and making it more intense and frequent than it really is, both of you can get a better perspective on it, and even see it as ridiculous.

The hug at the end is important to signal that the exercise is over and to acknowledge that you did not mean the abusive things you said. A few people who do this exercise have difficulty switching out of the anger mode. They may actually get upset and remain upset beyond the cutoff point. If you find this happening, the exercise isn't for you. Not every exercise is suitable for every couple.

USING A THIRD PARTY

As indicated in Trap #21, enlisting a third party to bolster your position against your partner is harmful. However, when both of you find it difficult to make headway on your own, participation by an outsider can be invaluable. A third party can serve a number of functions:

A) *Acting as an outside listener.* The likelihood of open hostility and other destructive irrationality is lessened, simply because a third party is physically present and listening.

B) *Acting as a relay.* In some instances it is so difficult for a couple to communicate that an intermediary may be helpful by relaying messages from one partner to the other. The principle here is similar to the technique of using written notes or even sending each other tapes, so that there is no direct verbal contact.

C) *Acting as an interpreter.* Rather than simply relaying messages, the third party may interpret the meaning of your communication, recast it in a more constructive way and then transmit it to your partner.

Florence:	"Bob is a stingy bastard."
Therapist:	(to Bob) "Jane would greatly appreciate it if you were somewhat freer about spending money."

D) *Mediating*. The third party may try to resolve certain issues by getting both of you to negotiate and by suggesting compromises. Often, he or she can help you work out contracts.

E) *Arbitrating*. The third party may, with the consent of both of you, make decisions that will be binding.

F) *Teaching communications skills*. The third party, especially if professionally trained, may teach and even supervise your practice of the skills that are necessary for getting along better.

G) *Treating illness*. The third party, a physician in this case, may administer medical treatment for conditions mentioned earlier that produce disruptive behavior, such as bipolar mood disorder (manic-depressive illness), premenstrual syndrome, temporal lobe epilepsy, and thyroid abnormalities.

In addition to the *functions* of a third party, his or her *qualities* are important. Among the attributes that are desirable in a third party are impartiality, that is, not favoring you or your partner, yet being free to agree or disagree with particular opinions or actions of either of you. A third party has to command the respect of both of you and also show respect for both of you. In addition, it is essential for the third party to distinguish his/her own needs from what is best for you. This person should be an effective communicator. He/she serves as a role model— an example of how to be assertive, how to listen, how to show respect, how not to be judgmental, how to recognize and respond to your positive qualities, and how to share his/her own experiences and opinions without being dogmatic.

Now that we've talked about the functions and qualities of the third party, the remaining issue is whom to choose? You may want a trained professional. Sometimes a friend or relative—or anyone who is trusted and respected by both of you and has the qualities listed above—will do. Rarely, I have seen older children who are spectacularly effective in that role, but, unless they are already doing it and it is helpful, they should not be put in such an awkward position.

What if you want to consult an outside person and your partner refuses? There are many reasons why people don't want to go to a therapist or other facilitator: they think it won't do any good; they are uncomfortable talking about intimate problems; they don't want to risk being blamed; they don't want to be branded as sick and in need of help; or, they think that people should be able to solve problems on their own and that seeking assistance is a sign of weakness. How should you deal with this resistance? The key is to make it as comfortable as possible for your partner to get involved. Don't blame or ridicule. It is often best to ask your partner to do it for your sake, rather than for her/his benefit or even for the relationship. You are distressed and you are asking your partner to help relieve your distress by going with you to a third party. In addition, it helps to ask your partner to go for one session only, so that there is no feeling of commitment to a prolonged course of therapy. If you have done all of this in a constructive way and your partner still won't join you, go to the therapist yourself. After the first visit, ask again and say that the therapist can best help you by getting your partner's viewpoint. If presented in a positive and non-threatening way, these arguments are usually successful. Occasionally, a friend, relative or even the therapist may be able to persuade your unwilling partner.

If you, yourself, are reluctant to consult a third party because you feel embarrassed about having problems, remember you are in the majority. The shame is not in having problems, but in wanting to get along better and not taking the necessary steps to *make it as a couple.*

CONCLUSION

Whether you try everything I have suggested or use just a single idea, whether you skimmed the book quickly or studied it in depth, here are the tools to create a better life for yourself and your partner. You need to look at your own actions, decide what you want, and follow the exercises that have worked for so many other couples. Remember the three part success formula: **Motivation; Awareness;** and **Tools.** Now that I've given you some ideas for *making it as a couple*, the next step is up to you.

APPENDIX				
ARE YOU AWARE OF DOING THIS?				
TRAP	PARTNER			
	A		B	
	YES	NO	YES	NO
1. RECITING PAST GRIEVANCES	☑	☐	☐	☐
2. DISAPPROVING	☑	☐	☐	☐
3. CRITICIZING	☑	☐	☐	☐
4. BLAMING & SELF-JUSTIFYING	☐	☐	☐	☐
5. MAKING ACCUSATIONS	☑	☐	☐	☐
6. INTERROGATING YOUR PARTNER	☑	☐	☐	☐
7. THREATENING	☐	☐	☐	☐
8. TAKING CREDIT	☐	☐	☐	☐
9. BEING RIGHT	☐	☐	☐	☐
10. REGRETTING	☐	☐	☐	☐
11. UNIVERSALIZING YOUR OWN OPINION	☑	☐	☐	☐

APPENDIX				
ARE YOU AWARE OF DOING THIS?				
TRAP	**PARTNER**			
	A		**B**	
	YES	NO	YES	NO
12. CONFUSING THE PERSON WITH THE DEED	☐	☐	☐	☐
13. USING A DOUBLE STANDARD	☐	☐	☐	☐
14. DISPLAYING NEGATIVE DRAMATIC BEHAVIOR	☐	☐	☐	☐
15. USING NEGATIVE EMOTIONAL LANGUAGE	☐	☐	☐	☐
16. USING VAGUE TERMS	☐	☐	☐	☐
17. TAKING MEANINGLESS ISSUES SERIOUSLY	☐	☐	☐	☐
18. USING PSYCHOLOGICAL WARFARE	☐	☐	☐	☐
19. MAKING NEGATIVE COMPARISONS	☐	☐	☐	☐
20. SAYING NO	☐	☐	☐	☐
21. APPEALING TO OR QUOTING THIRD PARTIES FOR SUPPORT	☐	☐	☐	☐

APPENDIX				
ARE YOU AWARE OF DOING THIS?				
TRAP	PARTNER			
	A		B	
	YES	NO	YES	NO
22. BEING INATTENTIVE	☐	☐	☐	☐
23. FAILING TO RESPOND POSITIVELY	☐	☐	☐	☐
24. INVALIDATING PARTNER'S PERCEPTION	☐	☐	☐	☐
25. PUNISHING THE POSITIVE	☐	☐	☐	☐
26. DOING A GOOD DEED, SOURLY	☐	☐	☐	☐
27. DEVALUING PARTNER'S CONTRIBUTIONS OR ACCOMPLISHMENTS	☐	☐	☐	☐
28. DEMANDING PURE MOTIVES	☐	☐	☐	☐
29. USING ALWAYS AND NEVER	☐	☐	☐	☐
30. EXTRACTING REASSURANCE	☐	☐	☐	☐
31. EXTRACTING COMMITMENTS	☐	☐	☐	☐
32. GIVING ADVICE WITHOUT BEING ASKED	☐	☐	☐	☐

APPENDIX				
ARE YOU AWARE OF DOING THIS?				
TRAP	PARTNER			
	A		B	
	YES	NO	YES	NO
33 GIVING ORDERS	☑	☐	☐	☐
34. ABUSING A CONFIDENCE	☐	☐	☐	☐
35. TALKING NEGATIVELY ABOUT YOUR PARTNER TO OTHERS	☐	☐	☐	☐
36. GETTING EVEN	☐	☐	☐	☐
37. MAKING EXCUSES	☐	☐	☐	☐
38. LYING	☐	☐	☐	☐
39. COMPULSIVE TRUTH-TELLING	☐	☐	☐	☐
40. BEING JEALOUS	☑	☐	☐	☐
41. TAKING THE IRRATIONAL PERSONALLY	☑	☐	☐	☐
42. FAILING TO ACCEPT RESPONSIBILITY FOR YOUR OWN FEELINGS	☐	☐	☐	☐

APPENDIX				
ARE YOU AWARE OF DOING THIS?				
TRAP	PARTNER			
	A		B	
	YES	NO	YES	NO
43. ATTACKING YOUR PARTNER'S BASIC RELATIONSHIPS	☑	☐	☐	☐
44. BEING OVERPROTECTIVE	☐	☐	☐	☐
45. SPEAKING FOR YOUR PARTNER	☐	☐	☐	☐
46. MAKING UNILATERAL DECISIONS	☐	☐	☐	☐
47. MAKING MALIGNANT INTERPRETATIONS	☑	☐	☐	☐
48. EXPLOITING YOUR PARTNER'S WEAKNESS	☑	☐	☐	☐
49. COMPLAINING	☑	☐	☐	☐
50. MAKING NEGATIVE PREDICTIONS	☑	☐	☐	☐
51. PREVENTING PARTNER FROM DOING WHAT'S IMPORTANT TO HIM/HER	☑	☐	☐	☐

APPENDIX				
ARE YOU AWARE OF DOING THIS?				
TRAP	PARTNER			
	A		B	
	YES	NO	YES	NO
52. MIND READING	☐	☐	☐	☐
53. ALLOWING OUTSIDE INTERFERENCE	☐	☐	☐	☐
54. PRETENDING TO WANT A BETTER RELATIONSHIP WHEN YOU DON'T	☐	☐	☐	☐

REFERENCES

* Alberti, R. & Emmons, M. *Your Perfect Right* (6th Ed.). San Luis Obispo, CA.: Impact Publishers, 1990.

§ Bandler, R. *Using Your Brain-For A Change*. Moab, Utah: Real People Press, 1985.

Beck, A.T. *Love Is Never Enough*. New York: HarperCollins, 1989.

Fay, A. *Making Things Better By Making Them Worse*. New York: Hawthorn, 1978. Distributed by FMC BOOKS, Essex, CT.

Fay, A. Sexual problems related to poor communication. *Medical Aspects of Human Sexuality*, June, 1977.

Fay, A. Sexual put-off: bringing up past grievances. *Medical Aspects of Human Sexuality*, November, 1983.

Gottman, J. *Why Marriages Succeed or Fail*. New York: Simon & Schuster, 1994.

* Jakubowski, P., & Lange, A.J. *The Assertive Option*. Champaign, IL: Research Press, 1978.

§ Lazarus, A. A. *In The Mind's Eye*. New York: Guilford Press, 1985.

Lazarus, A. A. *Marital Myths*. San Luis Obispo, CA: Impact Publishers, 1986.

Lazarus, A. A., & Fay, A. *I Can If I Want To*. New York: Warner, 1977.

McKay, M., Davis, M., & Fanning, P. *Messages*. Oakland, CA: New Harbinger Publications, 1983.

§ Singer, J.L., & Switzer, E. *Mind-Play*. Englewood Cliffs, NJ: Prentice-Hall, 1980.

§ Zilbergeld, B., & Lazarus, A.A. *Mind Power*. Boston: Little, Brown, 1987.

* Books about assertiveness
§ Books about imagery

About the author . . .

Allen Fay is a psychiatrist in private practice in New York City. He is a graduate of New York Medical College and completed his residency training in psychiatry at the Mount Sinai Hospital in New York. He is on the faculty of the Mount Sinai School of Medicine, where he teaches behavioral and cognitive approaches to therapy. Dr. Fay is a diplomate of The American Board of Psychiatry and Neurology. He is the author of *The Invisible Diet, Making Things Better By Making Them Worse* and co-author of *Don't Believe It For A Minute* and *I Can If I Want To.*

For additional copies of

Making it as a Couple

the perfect gift for anyone in a relationship,
or anyone who wants to be in a relationship that really works!

visit your local bookseller or complete this form
(or a photocopy) and return it to:

FMC BOOKS
P.O. Box 275
Essex, Connecticut 06426

··

Please send _____ copies of Making it as a Couple
at $12.95 each, plus $2.50 shipping and handling for the first book and
50¢ for each additional book being sent to the same U.S. address.
Connecticut residents add 6% sales tax.

(Quantity discounts apply: 5-11 copies 10% off; 12-20 copies 20% off.
For larger quantities, please write to the publisher.)

Name _____

Address _____

City _____ State _____ Zip _____

Please make checks and money orders payable to FMC Books.

BOOKSELLERS: STANDARD TRADE TERMS APPLY